**Other titles in the UWAP Poetry series
(established 2016)**

Leni Shilton's verse novel, *Walking with Camels* gives voice to the forgotten story of Bertha Strehlow and her intrepid journey into Central Australia in 1936. It traces her time with anthropologist and linguist, Ted Strehlow as they work with Indigenous communities there. In highlighting her side of their relationship, and reanimating her sometimes life-threatening experiences, Shilton explores and questions various kinds of silence connected to the lives of Australian women and evokes a powerful sense of Australian country and landscape. This is a compelling poetic narrative that opens new perspectives onto the past.

Paul Hetherington

This compelling verse novel offers a powerful evocation of the life of Bertha Strehlow, centering on the years she spent with her husband, Ted Strehlow, in Australia's Central Desert region. Throughout, it is her voice we hear, its tone both calm and passionate, as she recounts the initial ordeal of adaptation to vast treks through desert country, then the miscarriage of her first child and the dangerous illness that results; many further trials will follow. However, the novel also traces the revelatory and transforming nature of Bertha's encounter with the desert region at the heart of Australia, and her attunement to the generosity and spiritual understandings of the Aboriginal people she travels with, or encounters.

Leni Shilton's re-imagining of Bertha Strehlow's life, grounded in deep research, is informed by a beautifully measured empathy. She shows us Bertha's heroic endurance in the face of great physical and emotional pain, ('I bleed life / and regret / nothing'), and her courageous openness to life and its gifts. And there are moments of lightness, as when Bertha dances under 'the silken sky', or sings while swimming in a waterhole.

The unfolding narrative of *Walking with Camels* is rendered in skilfully shaped poetic monologues and lyrics notable for their naturalness and authenticity. Leni Shilton achieves at times a luminous clarity in speaking of the desert country, and there is a sense of both warmth and wonder at its creatures, including those fascinating ring-ins, the camels. Walking with Camels is a richly inspiring work which touches into the resonant silences of the desert, while breaching another kind of silence to tell the moving story of Bertha Strehlow.

Diane Fahey

Walking with Camels

Leni Shilton

Leni Shilton is a poet, nurse, educator who has worked in Aboriginal adult education in the Northern Territory for 25 years. After growing up in Melbourne and Rabaul, Papua New Guinea, Leni settled in Alice Springs where she focused her writing on people, place and identity. She has twice won the Northern Territory Literary Poetry and Essay Awards, and in 2015 was shortlisted in the University of Canberra Poetry Prize. In February 2016 she completed a PhD in creative writing. Her writing has appeared in anthologies and journals in Australia and internationally. She is the recipient of creative writing grants and international residencies and her work has appeared in exhibitions and adapted for the stage. Leni is a founding member of Ptilotus Press, a small publishing initiative which promotes central Australian writing. She currently works for the Ngaanyatjarra Pitjantjatjara Yankunytjatjara Women's Council in Alice Springs, where she supports violence prevention programs.

Leni Shilton
Walking with Camels
The story of Bertha Strehlow

First published in 2018
and reprinted in 2020 by
UWA Publishing
Crawley, Western Australia 6009
www.uwap.uwa.edu.au

UWAP is an imprint of UWA Publishing
a division of The University of Western Australia

 A catalogue record for this
book is available from the
National Library of Australia

Designed by Becky Chilcott, Chil3
Typeset in Lyon Text by Lasertype
Printed by Lightning Source

This project has been assisted by the Australian
Government through the Australia Council, its arts
funding and advisory body.

 uwapublishing

To Deb Westbury
Poet, mentor, dearest friend

Contents

Note on orthography and units of measure

The Arrernte orthography throughout this work uses the historical Hermannsburg spelling of 'Aranda'. I have not sought to correct the spelling of place names, or to change miles to kilometres; these remain as cited in the original texts.

Chapter 1

Beginnings

1934–1936

At the dance

I'd heard about him –
the smart one, born in the desert,
making the languages of Central Australia his own.
He is shy, handsome and dances well.

His accent is polished, but I hear the German
reach through his voice
when I tell him an old flame has married.
His heart so open, so red raw
I want to cover it.

I tell him she's a fool.
'I wouldn't let you
slip through my fingers.'

He stops mid-step,
the music rolling around us,
he has just seen me
for the first time.

Heart of darkness

I tell my university friends
I'm going, leaving.
'With him?'
'Yes – off on an adventure!'

They can't see past the strangeness
of my frowning fiancé,
and look worried.

I aim to have a wonderful time
and tell them so;
'It will be like
going into the heart of darkness
in my own
country.'

Maps

My finger traces the line snaking
to the Centre,
the map, a pattern of unfamiliar marks
across vast spaces.
'Where will we live?' I ask Ted.

He points at strange names,
his finger rests on dots
on the yellowed paper.
'Here or here,
there is much work to be done.'

My hands shake
but his strength,
his belief
steadies me.

Adelaide

December 1935

I have lived my life
perched at the edge
of brown peninsulas
that push like arrows into
the still waters of the gulf
and the Southern Ocean,
where the falling sun
drops orange into western seas.

Where the green hills of Adelaide
lean away from
city streets
and the pale stone of churches,
reminders of Empire.

I am leaving,
my back to straight streets
and cold hills.
Walking from my father's door
with the sureness of youth
not yet understanding doubt,
but knowing there is
nothing I will recognise
in the desert.

Counselling

I remember one day after church
the minister took me aside:
'There might be some difficulties,' he said.
I'm startled
and it must have shown.

'Of faith...' He reddened,
'but at least he's a Protestant,
a Catholic would have been just too difficult.'

'Sorry, do you mean because he's a Lutheran?'
'Yes, and from missionary stock...German
they look at things...differently,
there's all that work with the blacks...'

Through the sun-filled window,
the green of the elm
caught the light,
and I just waited
for the interview to be over.

The train

The sea pulls away from me,
a vast retreating tide
as the train grinds north,
climbing the map
into heat.

The towns grow smaller,
until they are little more than
a sprinkling of people
huddled at rail sidings.
As far as the eye can see –
red rocks dot
the flat plains.

The windows jam with dust,
crawl with flies
my throat clots with hot air,

but my new husband and I
gaze out the clouded window,
hold hands,
and when no one looks
he kisses me.

Alice Springs

18th February 1936

The town is one street.
Fences pushed into red sand
Whites in houses,
natives in reserves.
I step in dirt.

At the hostel,
the nursing sisters
make tea
and gossip.
The most exciting news –
Olive Pink is back in town
for a truck, a driver and provisions.
Her next plan
to live in the north-west,
study the Warlpiri.
Ted stomps, furious
and I change the subject.

By the next day we are gone –
our bags caked in dust
in the back of the mission truck.

To Father
from Hermannsburg

My first view of the mission
was through a blanket of dust.
The storm lasted for days.
Kind missionaries gave us a home
to stay in.
Black helpers fed us,
served tea in the parlour,
fine china on lace cloths.
The older black women
are still called girls.

The missionaries
speak highly of Ted's parents,
their many years of work here.

We felt the suspicion
from some in Alice Springs,
but here, we are at home in Ted's birth place
this strange Lutheran Aranda world
is his true home.

At Pastor Albrecht's
the dinner discussion ran in circles;
is it more important to save souls
than to write down
language?
Can you do one without the other?

Ted does love to hold the floor,
and there really is nothing he doesn't know
about this place.
Later in our room
he paced the stone floor,
angry as he heard
of more mistreatment of the Aranda,
the latest shootings,
the deaths.
People are only safe
on the Mission.

We are leaving soon
on the trek –
Ted has marked the route
on the map,
many miles west and south of here.
We'll take camels
and some black helpers.

The mail is not reliable.
You won't get this until we are
in deep desert.
I think of you often
Your daughter,

Bertha
Hermannsburg 1936

Panic

I wake in black darkness
and rising panic,
no street lights to puncture the dark.
I wait for my sleeping brain to clear.

Until I wake enough,
to the moment
of remembering
where I am.

Heat

In the dark and stillness of the night
when the buzz seems to have gone from his head,
when he has settled,
we find each other
we are one: hands, faces
given up to the heat.

Trek

'This trek across country
it may take many months,'
Ted grins as he tells me.

He is a dusty man,
a squat-by-the-campfire man
his clothes creased with dirt,
boots moulded to his feet.
The thought of travel brings him joy,
our lumpy bed at the mission
not rough enough for him.

Camels

Animals from picture books
stand as tall as the house.

I'm not frightened at first
I don't know
what to be frightened of

but they spit and snort
and bellow
and smell of something uncivilised.

Over time I will grow to love them –
when they carry me across
deserts –
saving me.

I am not easily frightened
and I feel Ted's gaze on me.

The locals are watching me too,
all eyes on the new bride.

So I smile,
my hand in the thick fur
I make myself enjoy the company
of these creatures.

Photographs

My husband is one for photographs.
He has hundreds in boxes,
and more sent off
to this university and that.
People think
that Aboriginal people are disappearing,
he is documenting a fading world.

I know he fears for his old childhood friends
he wants to save them from the winds of change
that sweep the desert.

His photographs
and his writings, his maps
hold onto an ancient world.
Is he wasting his time,
will the people be gone?

I ask him,
will writing their words
help them move into this world,
this different civilisation?

Music

I know his fingers are itching
for music,
so when he finds the old organ
in the sitting room
of his childhood house,
we hear his talent
all over the Mission.
It is the organ
his father
paid £5 for in 1896,

yellowed keys
and stained wood,
the sound is still joyful,
as he settles into the rhythm
of the music.

The gramophone

May 1936

The music moves against the canvas.
I am dancing,
my skirt could be silk
and my shoes
fine sandals.

He holds me, murmurs in my ear.
I try and remember
what it was he said,
to make me leave my green hills –
my parents.

He spoke in coloured dreams
that turned my head –
stories of nomads and deserts.

Spoke in a language that
rose and fell –
an ancient music.

It could have been Africa
we were coming to,
a more different world
I couldn't imagine.

The gramophone
is a link
to my old life,
and here I dance with him –

my feet in thick shoes,
stepping lightly
through the dust.

Camel boxes

The clink of metal
comes to me through
the open window
I follow the sound to the forge
to Ted –
blackened with soot
his face red in the heat.

He grins, holds up hot metal
in gloved hands, 'These
are for the camel boxes.'
'Oh good,' I say,
hoping he will explain later.

After days of hammering and painting
the finished products are very handsome:
green timber boxes
in metal frames
to strap to each side of our camels.

I understand now –
the camels and their strength
are our lifeline.

Gone

He is ever keen to be gone;
eager for his feet to be
moving as fast as his brain,
his mouth,
and his pen.

The camels are much too slow
but they are all we have.
Some days he will walk ahead of them,
striding off into the distance.
We come up behind
our slow lope the wrong rhythm for him.

Chapter 2

Walking with camels

1936

The eye of a needle

The camels stride –
a fine string
through the trees.
Cliffs rise red
over the gap
and the line of camels,
thread themselves through
one, two, three
until they are gone.

Voices echo
from inside
the gap:
Aranda men calling
camel commands
in Arabic –
the rocks speak
as clouds lick at cliff tops.

The camels tread
with ease
through the country,
and I am reminded
strangely,
of rich men and the eye of a needle.

Rain

The day darkens, turns to rain.
We walk in fine mist,
the sand deepened to blood red,
until we are wet through.

Poetry reading

By a kerosene lamp late into the night,
we read poetry.
My husband's favourite:
TS Eliot.
Shape without form, shade without colour
Paralysed force, gesture without motion

We read of the destruction of the world
as the sky fades in streaks of red
and the bleeding clouds
follow the line of the curved horizon.

The end of the world
feels far from here;
a breeze blows in from the west,
stars pull themselves through,
and the white slither moon
falls into the darkening earth.

We read aloud –
him, then me.
I want to read words of love,
but his poetry fills the air
with its threats of hollow men
marching through death dreams.

I shudder in the emptiness,
wonder if this is how God sees us:
two people in a vast desert,

our words becoming the wind
as we speak
into the voiceless night.

The silence

This dark night
desert air reaches
beyond the humanness
of this place.

It is an aching silence
that pulses
with expectation and destruction.

All our walking
in 'undiscovered country'
becomes discovery of
emptiness,
of silence.

Midnight thinking is black
and as the tent walls
flex and stretch,
I wish I was somewhere else.

Hoppity

Ted's red face
appears over the sand
that piles up as he digs,

his arm disappearing into creek sand.
'There!' he says. 'I've found water!'

I take the joey to him so it can drink
but it turns from Ted,
thin arms clawing the air
as it hops its way back to me.

Grains of mica stick to Ted's face,
glint in the light,

he drops in the sand
his head in his hands,

the rejection of this small creature
fills him with despair.

The ghosts at Horseshoe Bend

The cold sets
in our bones
and even the locals can't stand it.

I get down from the camel
to walk out of the wind.

By the time we stop
the wind has dropped
and we sit at the campfire
warming in silence,
just the bells of the camels
calling from across the creek.

A long night, aching cold
in the riverbed
and at daybreak
the water in the
billy is ice.

The cliffs near Horseshoe Bend
glow red in the morning,
frowning at us.

We pack, move on
the wind
pushing at our back
again.

Alone with the language

At the campfire,
the only woman

the only one growing a child,
the only one who hears
a new language
every passing day.

No one understands me
in the silence
of the bush,
with no one to talk to
and no one who will listen.

Morning sick

I hadn't told him,
but he knows when my breakfast
comes up morning after morning.
He talks about going back.
Is it safe
walking the desert
in this condition?
My hands go to my belly,
as if to cover the baby's ears,
lest we frighten it.

I am growing accustomed
to the new being
that grows in me
making me as sick
as if I was at sea.

I don't yet know
that it knows everything,
even my thoughts.

Patterns

Footsore we unpack
knowing
it will be hours before we can rest.

But the end of the day
has its calming patterns.

The men unpack the camels,
I gather branches,
start the fire
and ready the meal
for Ted to cook.

Ancient light

The sky poured with milk,
a crowd of stars
silken cold held in
blue black at the horizon.

The air
alive with stars
that stream across
the darkening bowl.

Night after night
this ancient light,
a bedtime story
read in pictures.

Late afternoon

The late sun shines silver in the grass fields,
in the stretch of spinifex sprouting after rain.
It has the look of fertile country
but it's not.

As the wind dips, the quiet whispers in my ears.
All the world is here
under the falling sun,
the country a gift of light and softening air.

I hear the sound of night being called in,
camels, kettles,
the fire coming to life,
the smell of evening smoke resting in the valley.

Evening cold lifts from the creek bed,
I tend to the fire, the cooking,
let the yellow light
touch my pale skin,
in the final warmth
of late afternoon.

Rage

The mind of a man is a mystery to me,
oh, I understand much,
the power of desire –
I am young yet
and understand passion still.

It is the solitary fight
against the universe
I don't understand,
the rage against God and man
that separates
my husband from the rest of us.

I see him in my mind's eye at his happiest
as a dot on the landscape by a small fire;
note book in one hand, and pen in the other.

Mt Connor

(Found poem)

At night the camp fire
burns to bright coals,
and the bush stillness
is marked only by
the curlew and mopoke.

George tells stories of demons
living in the west,
the country we are walking to.

He says they look like cats
they spring on travellers,
tear them to pieces.

All the people have gone
there is no one out there
but dead men's bones
he says.

Night falls cold

August 1936

The night falls cold again.
It has been two months now
I am long past the worry
of bush bathrooms –
it is all part of life.

Dingoes call their strange howl,
sounding close, no matter the distance.
Creatures scratch the canvas
and the wind brushes the tent walls.

Ice coats the basin, the kettle,
and my swag
as the cold creeps in.

Speaking country

The way the country speaks to you:
in the wind
the drift of smoke from the camp fire,
the dry leaves over sand,
the glow of the morning.

The country has a way of speaking,
of making the rest of the world drift away,
until it is only here
that matters.

Chapter 3

Into the west –
the Petermann Ranges

1936

Inland Sea

The Inland Sea
lies rotting.
Mile upon mile
of rock, stone.
The people gone,
lingering confused
at the distant shores.

Haircutting at Piltadi

We have stopped,
camels tethered;
their bells echo about the bush
like the memory of forest birds.

The weather being mild, we unpack;
do the washing,
and with all that we own in the world
marking our place in the sand,
we take turns at haircutting.

I do quite a style on Ted's
and later, tidy up
the bits he missed
of mine.

The peace stretches here,
and we speak in whispers
as we spread into the desert.

Mt McCulloch

Today we saw a hill
in the shape of a fallen camel.
It lay restful on the plain,
but we shuddered as we walked by,
and didn't look back
lest the idea attached itself to us too firmly.

My husband is looking for three men,
Witchetty saw their footprints yesterday
'naked men' as George calls them.
Today I keep camp as the men travel on quick camels
following their quarry.

But the naked men are fast,
lighting small fires to cook,
keep their firebrands alight
then moving on
their footprints, a travelling story.

The country grows as lines,
a map in Ted's diary –
Piltadi, Mt Bowley, Piltadi again.
It is the last water for many days,
and hard to turn away from.

I cook for Ted
keep the fire friendly for me.
I know now I am unwell,
and wait, uneasy.

He returns as the day ends,
as it turns to dark, he unrolls the swag
and I rest.

He straightens the camp
washes out our dishes,
makes bread, tinkers with the fire.

The setting sun throws shadows past the fallen camel hill –
another rise for Ted to mark on his map.
Tomorrow, he will search again,
for the running men.

Reading the sand

Today
Ted camps
down the creek-bed,
talking with the three old men
George has found.

Ted asks about white explorers.
'Did they shoot four countrymen?'
George translates Ted waits,
Pitjantjatjara into Aranda,
Aranda into Pitjantjatjara,
back and forth.

The old men are trackers –
readers of the sand.
They know who has passed through their land:
what they ate and drank,
the direction they were heading,
where they might be now.
But the old men shake their heads,
their hands –
there's no trace of the lost men,
not a footprint.

They talk nervously of spirits,
eyes flick at the waterhole,
worry in their voices,
speak of the missing men
in quick whispers.

Kungkarrangkalpa

– Stories of the Seven Sisters

George talks to me today
no longer shy.
But never do his eyes meet mine,
he stands beside me
and we look west.

Hands busy and with few words,
he explains the travels of the Seven Sisters –
who were chased by the ancestor,
the journey
making the waterholes and the hills.
'This part I can tell you' he adds.

Because of the stories, (his hands tell me)
the people are firm on the ground.
They command the air with their song,
telling the stories of here –
in the shape of the mountains,
the run of sand on the riverbed,
a secret waterhole cut into rock.

My husband is busy
with the camel boxes and straps
and when he looks up,
George has returned to his work
gathering in the camels.
He calls to them in Arabic
and the ring of bells follows him
through the mulga.

Later, as shadows lengthen
and trail long behind us,
the wind in the desert oak
is a whisper like words from the past,
and I am sure I can feel the sisters still.

Camping east of Mt Philips

The flies are here today.
The bush buzzes with their whine.

The wind is cool at my back
but the sun burns if I stray out of the shade,
'winter–summer' days Ted calls them.
We are forever putting on jumpers
then pulling them off again.

In the still space
further talk is unnecessary.
We sit together in the buzz of quiet,
drink tea.

The crows call across the river
telling each other of our activities,
I feel sure they are laughing at us.
They wing away over country
we still have to trudge through.

Rippled clouds stretch
long white lines over the horizon,
in patterns like beach sand.

The crows return
take up residence in the gums above us.
We are new to the neighbourhood
so they check on us
their heads tilting with yellow eyes.

Budgerigars chatter on, invisible in the grey gums,
rocks at the waterhole glow red as the day ends,
and in the fading light blush brighter.

Something unseen
disturbs the budgerigars
they lift *en masse* to another tree,
chirrup in circling laughter.

He tells me I am calmer here,
I laugh, tell him there is not much to be done.
I begin to see country:
like the hills to the south that look like a fallen camel.
he tells me this is a way
of letting the country in.

Even as my body drains
life away,
today is a good day.

I know he has always had this,
the country always being in him.
From the moment his Aranda mother
took him in her arms, spoke to him in her language.
From that moment he was forever part of here
in a way I never can be.

Mt Bowley

Our journey
ended
at Mt Bowley
near the Shaw River,
a fine broad creek bed,
and we passed close by
Winter's Glen
where Lasseter
is buried

We had hoped
we might
have a baby next year

but
it is not to be,
not to be.

Nothing

The days pass
me, bleeding life.

I write to Father,
try a cheery letter:

> The country spreads vast,
> empty.

But the cramps get Ted's attention
and his loving eyes crease
with concern.

> The waterholes are green, low, edges pushed in
> by nervous cattle. The other day I saw a calf,
> its thin flank shaking as it nudged the bones of its
> mother.

Ted tends to me, feeds me,
his hands almost tender.

> We have named the camels, each for its personality
> it's like travelling with a group of children one day
> and grumpy old women the next.
> They calm us though; stride through the country as if
> it is theirs.

Ted's eyes are better than any mirror,
and I say my prayers.

> Father, I am so lucky to have seen this country,
> so lucky to have your love,
> your loving daughter
> forever.

I bleed life
and regret
nothing.

Beauty

4th September 1936

Beauty is a young man
so filled with fear and passion
he breathes his secrets to me.

Here the desert sky
reaches beyond the heavens.
It presses down on us and
he speaks of loss –
of being utterly alone,
and we pray
that God will save us.

I feel calm – safe
we confess old secrets
our sins punished

we are here alone –
our baby gone now.

Her tiny, hardly formed body
buried by the tree
where I have cried myself empty.

And my stained
towels colour the waterhole pink
I watch him,
bent by the sand
as he washes them.
There is no one else.

At the waterhole

8th September 1936

I will write to my mother-in-law,
tell her,
but for now I must go on,
get well, and look after my dear husband.

I started bleeding
weeks ago,
at first I thought it might just be the heat
and the long days of walking –
we covered thirty miles yesterday,
but I know now that the baby has gone.

I cried when I told my love,
he was sad, but sensible,
We'll have more.
And I agreed, because I know we will,
but as I bleed and the strength goes out of me
I worry about what this means for the future.

The men with us
are as awkward
as my husband.
They know there's women's business going on
and have camped far away.

How I miss being with women,
they would have washed my bloodied rags,
cared for me in that gentle way of women.

Ted is making a litter of sorts –
a stretcher for the side of the camel,
a frame to carry me back to civilisation.
It keeps him busy
and although he works quite nearby
I am quite alone with my loss.

I dreamt of the baby last night –
a girl, and in the dream, she was quite grown.
She was swimming in the waterhole
her skin gleamed.
She called for me to join her
but I just waved
and stayed sitting on the sandy banks.

If I speak from under the earth

I speak from under the earth, the desert a red beast over me. History is layers of time on my voice; broken sand, dust air and cloud blur. The sky pushes into me until the life I had before this moment dries up, gone on hot wind. I remember when I didn't know the desert was owned; spoken for. I was young then – earnest. Travellers still stumble over, and in, call it empty, choose not to see beings in every rock, every hill. *Can you see it?* The shape of the mountains there – they say it's the ancestors walking, making the stories. I know now that the people are sick – see that crying country! I hear them call. Cattle trample the waterhole – edges falling in and the camels afraid to reach their long necks to green water. *Listen!* The birds are silent at the rockhole, the dingo, thin like a hopeful shadow, presses soft steps on the ground, its body yellow as sand. The air waits; rising smoke folds in a white line from the creek bed. I wait also, my day follows the passing clouds, the sun. The shape of my body lying in the sand makes valleys for the colonies of ants. Mica specks shine on my skin: this is the moment I love, the desert warm on me; the day slow, I sleep. When I wake, the cold creeps through the sand from ground-water deep below. The night a black blanket I can't find the edge of, the dingoes call loneliness in the dark; they cry like they are hurting and I shiver knowing people die here. The mopoke calls late and distant from across the hills. *Can you feel it?* I must speak from under the earth to be heard, with a voice no longer mine. The desert is its own animal, alone and desperate. *Enough* it snarls, barely glancing at me as it performs its night ritual. The stars save me, their distant glowing buzz a thick light like white paint splitting the sky. My night dreams wander; here I see the stories, the land maps that roll across the country, and it is a comfort.

The women

They step out of the dark,
their black skin
mixing with the night,
and we don't know
until the firelight
picks up their eyes.

They are frightened;
of our camels, of us,
but they leave me
with herbs
to stop my bleeding.

I watch,
as if through fog.

Skies and waterholes

The sky bloodied,
a reflection of the waterhole.
The crimson sky our only warning
and we take what God hands out.

I hold onto the journey
as an adventure:
that is what I will tell the children,
when I am old,
when they have grown,
when I survive.

I know people die out here;
I've read of the explorers
by the crystal lakes –
salt like ice,
a white that never melts.

I fall in and out of death
my mind so full.
I thought I would be years older,
I thought I would have done more.
Have taught – sung more?
I sing so well.
But not now;
my voice
has gone into weeping.
Now black faces
stare at me.

The women are here,
tall, black, thin,
so thin!
What do they eat
when there is no food in these lands?

From those who have nothing –
no clothes, no lizards hanging from the hairstring
at their waists,
no children,
no husbands, not here at least;
they give me herbs,
and it is from
their land that I am saved.

Flossie

Flossie is my favourite.
She knows my voice,
looks up when I am nearby,
and I'm sure her face
is softer than the others,
eyes warmer.

Now I lie in the stretcher
strapped to her side –
rock to and fro
with each step.

The bitter dung
in my nose,
hair, my skin.
The damp towel
over my face cools me
but the smell stays.

I close my eyes,
imagine I am comfortable,

for if we are ever to leave this place
she has to carry me out.

The Olgas

From first light we see them –
pink on the horizon,
their heads tilted down
leaning in
talking to themselves.

All day we travel,
and they grow
as we hope against hope
each red dune is the last.

But from the east a cold wind
splinters our clothes,
and the domes look like vanishing
into the plain of spinifex
before we reach them.

The first white woman

Bertha Strehlow, on seeing Ayers Rock, September 1936

I should say something at this moment –
the immense wonder of it,
its ancient form reaching above the flat plains,
a solidness on the ground
curled like a giant animal
that has slept for a millennium.

As we come into its folds
the western sun is blocked,
but I am too sick to notice light fall
on red rock,
now orange, now mauve.

I pray for many sunsets in this place.
I will record them with eloquence,
but in this moment I am ill, tired,
and grateful for the clear waters
at the rock's base,
an icy balm on my fevered lips,
I sleep safe in deep shadows.

Sound

A falling stone
rattles from the cliff
and me, alone at the waterhole
listening.
I must write the beauty onto the page,
but the pen is a dead weight
in my hand, and the book
is part of the ground.

I listen for his return;
I pray not to be alone
for long.
If I call, will he hear me?
But my strangled throat
twists in its tube.

I might die here,
for love, for beauty
and the moment would pass
so quietly.

The birds still at the water;
ants, lizards.
The moment gone –
soft, small,
a whisper
barely heard.

Chapter 4

Six years in Jay Creek

1937–1942

Dear Mother

Hermannsburg

8th October 1936

We are back again
at last,
from our long trek
out bush.
I suppose you have been
anxiously waiting for news.

I am quite well again now,
we felt always
that God was watching us
protecting us,
Ted will write, but he is ill
and can't make this mail.

We have not told anyone
else except my people
about the nature of my illness.
I know you will not mention it,
because the nature of Ted's position
will bring about plenty of
unfriendliness towards us and
we don't want to give people
the opportunity
to criticise us.
We want to keep our affair private
I know you will understand.
With much love from
Bertha Strehlow

The tent

The thin tent wall –
more a metaphor for a home
than an actual home.

Creatures visit,
they don't understand metaphors.
We block up holes and gaps
but ants and lizards
move through them,
and this morning I shuddered to see
the curved tracks
of a snake in the dust
beside my bed.

Journals

Each day he writes,
until
boxes line our tent.
Some days it's all he does,
letters to the Administrator,
the mission,

then his diary.

I laugh and tell him
one day
he will have
a library built in his honour
to keep them all.

Outhouse

My journey to the
outhouse –
a hazardous joy
the cold an aching.
I move in
quiet dark,
torch light waving
as even lizards
sleep.

And each night I
remember to look up,
for above me the
world opens.

Back in bed
my face cold on
Ted's warmth,
I can't help
my smile, wide
in the dark.

The horses at Jay Creek

I hear them in the night
stamping the ground
at my tent.
They trip on ropes
in the dark
and the tent slackens.

Sleek and lean
reflecting doubles
of themselves
in the waterhole at dusk.
The whole country
is copied golden
in thick toffee,
until ripples of their
drinking
roll like echoes
over and over
across the water.

Dream language

The Language felt in the rocks,
on the air through grey leaves.

A land language I hear on my skin
as it moves like a veil over my face.

Sound that touches under skin
like water seeping through sand,

that birds know before it is sound.
A scent cushioned on wind, on currents over hills,

in cloud,
in rain when it finds itself falling.

The flick of a bird's wing,
dust that falls as it turns.

And light, ragged on the horizon
brushed orange in the mountain's profile,

a misted rainbow of colour
fading to dark, with dotted stars –

lanterns to guard the cold night.
All sound, like a long held note.

The language fades from my ears,
but echoes loud in the land.

I move through rock,
creep in the dark, watch the night animals come.

The dark a type of home,
a tranquil breath

of giving in,
giving up, giving over.

A small moment
where all others wash off
into dreams
and I stop worrying for the first time.

Burning

He comes in breathless
speaking in statements –
it seems his sponsor has pulled out,
how will he find another?
He paces up and down in the tent – swearing.
Hush, I say, think of those around.

For a moment he has violence in his eyes,
the passion of indignation
burning out of them.

I'm sure we'll find another, I say,
knowing full well he has
burnt most bridges.

The pacing starts again:
red faced,
fists tight balls at his side.

He is like a moth
throwing himself
over and over
against the flame
waiting to catch fire.

113° F

Static air
and we drive,

the hills open
to a brown valley,
and a windmill creaking through
its cycle, the lumbering roll
drags a pole and water from
the ground, slime
troughs, the only green life.
Cattle yards are powder,
pressed by a thousand hooves.
Grey and pink
galahs wheel in, crowding the air.

We pull up
let the dust wave pass
get out and walk,
shading our eyes against the sun.

And outside the car, in the silence,
is the sound of distance.

Shifting dirt
and heat
our travelling companions.

Fire

The day started well;
bright and clear across the valley.
Then, a wind from the west,
and the smudge of smoke stain
clouded the day.
Time spent in worry,
and, at its end, we watch the
sunset spread fire across the sky.
In the morning the red
sunrise –
a warning for distant shepherds.

Small things

This day, the silence rests in small things:
the scratch of a leaf on rock,
the beat of air on bird wings,
the pull of the wind.
The lifting sky,
and the open drift of clouds.

The straight line of ants' trails
on sand
swept clean by constant traffic,

and at the edge of the waterhole,
the lap of tiny waves,
like the sound of lips
opening to a smile.

The movement of canvas
that is somehow a sound even
on the stillest of days.

Distant voices,
the possibility of a car,
the call of children,
and my empty weeping womb:
silence in the
smallest of things.

Songs of Central Australia

I
There is mourning in the camp.
Awake,
I listen to the rise and fall of weeping,
to the rhythm.

Later, I will tend to the wounds
made from rocks and sticks.
Now I weep in silence
for only those closest
can cry loudest.

II
The missionaries asked the people not to wail,
being German they were very strict about this.
All life events should be carried out as quietly,
as respectfully as possible.
Does quiet mean respect in German?

III
The women are singing
a Lutheran hymn in Aranda,
the lift of harmonies
not unlike weeping.

IV
At the rockhole
I slip from my clothes
alone,

I sing like I'm the only one in church
and my voice echoes back to me
from the rocks
clear and loud.

V
Birds call to the coming rain
their song, a warning;
I take the washing in,
tighten the tent against leaks
and the gathering clouds.

Walking east

The old woman from the camp
told me
which way to go:

Back over the hills
and into the valley
before the ranges –
you mustn't go

She says all this with
a point
of her finger
a flick of the wrist.
So I head east
along the road,
talcum powder dust
coating my shoes.

Above, an eagle floats in wide arcs
its shadow shape
frozen still
against the sky,

and at the road's edge
golden spiral flowers
drip with honey,
and glisten green
after the rain.

As I walk, red dust clouds bloom,
lifted from a car on the horizon.
Off the road
hills dip
like the small curves
of a woman's back.
Orange grasshoppers
fly from the spinifex
at each step.

As the sun shifts in the sky,
falling to the west,
the shadows stretch long
from the hills.

I try to imagine this country
in ten, fifteen, twenty years,
and fear only the jagged
spine of the mountain range
and the pattern of the travelling sun
will remain the same.

To Hermann Vogelsang, Point Pass

11th December 1937

Ted has today written
to a fellow missionary's son.
Like kindred spirits
they were born on the mission field
and raised with Aranda and Dieri in their ears.
Before German,
before English.

And like linked souls
wandering the desert
they come back again
and again to Aboriginal land –

The Dieri of Coopers Creek
have faded
their songs running
to a slow trickle
before melting into the sand.

So he comes,
now looking
for Aranda to serve.

Language lessons

Two girls come each day,
bold
they look at picture books,
laugh and point.
I listen to their Aranda
but my attempts
send them laughing more.

Living with Ted
who spoke
Aranda first
is no help to me.

He sits with the old men
writes down stories,
just as his father did –
writes in Aranda
to his mother in Germany.
She writes back in German.

I try to find the words,
to talk to the girls;
not understanding the sounds I hear,
I let them laugh.

Maggie

She arrived on a Thursday
a month after the flurry of letters.
Nineteen, TB of the larynx
A half caste, her baby
in the Half Caste Home.

We have asked and asked for
more provisions for her.
But it appears a waterproof sheet
is not justified.

Late in the night cold
I see her outside our tent,
her fire a small spot of light.

Weaving hands

They wanted me here
to wait for the baby
but no one speaks.
I wonder if I imagined the invitation
or dreamt it?

Hand signs around the campfire:
words of silence
through the air,
someone here from Hermannsburg?
old Jack gone to Alice Springs?
Mary clucks and chuckles
as if she knows it's a bad move for Jack.

This is quiet talk
happening with eyes
and weaving hands

As lives are taken over
by church and state,
this is quiet defiance.
In the spotted shade
on the dirt,
women wait
for the baby.

The birth

The air is pierced
by a soft grunt
and the head is in my hands –
too late for gloves.

She lets out a rush of air,
a frown lowers over her eyes
in grim focus
as her baby is born,
slippery and hard to hold.

Tiny brown arms fly
like she's falling,
eyes wide with surprise
at the sudden chill
and hard light.

But she takes to the nipple
like she knows,
eyes blinking
in a memory,
like a lens shutter.
The picture of her mother.

No sound from either,
their cocoon of silence
like a held breath.

And I see the blood.

She bleeds –
doesn't stop.
I lean my hands
into her soft empty belly
but she grows lighter –
the loss
a surprise to her.
Her eyes look at me:
What is this now?

And her baby
cries
like she knows.

First born

My body swells
this time
holding on
to the blood mass
cradled in me.

Doctors orders:
six months in bed,

so I stay and
watch as he goes,
the first of many leavings.

How is it that
a marriage
longs for children,
weeps over their loss,

but is divided by them?

The first crack

A car door wakes me,
a diesel engine.
Outside the day has not
yet started
and he is gone.
Where to this time?

Later I see the note:
Back in two weeks – Canberra, Ted.
I don't recall discussing this one.

The day breaks over the hills
and light floods
my room
warning of heat.

A crack is appearing
and I am unsure
how to stop it.

At the end of the frost

Another windy, cloud filled day
but I feel sure the frost is over.

Up early
and the air is warmer,
the ice breath of last week
past now.

The sun comes late to the day
but we are grateful and sit in warmth
in the lee of the breeze.

There, with cup of tea in hand
you tell me it is over
you are called to the army,
that we are to leave
to travel south.

Strange how it feels too soon.
I shiver
and try to imagine
my life without this desert in it.

Chapter 5

The dream

1942–1987

Writing distance

In the cool of the afternoon
I write.
I am too busy in the mornings
and too weary at night.
I know Ted is writing too
far from me in the desert –
it is as if we are a wide ocean
apart.

As voices drift in from the street,
I write to picture the place
no photo can do justice to.
Of the cold,
the silver crystals of ice in the kettle
on winter mornings.
Of the people whose language and ways
are as ancient as
the mountains and the valleys.

Of the wide black of the sky
at night,
the light of stars,
like a hundred thousand candles
dotting the blackness.

The dream

takes me to hidden rock walls –
rubbed smooth
pink and translucent.
My hand runs the cool stone
where water flows.
It is old here
like the chanting stories
my husband writes.
I hear singing
in the walls like water,
like the deluge
that never comes.

The dream is warm sand
cold rock and red quartz.
I stay here
safe in the wide arms
of old country.
As small birds twitter
in delight at the waterhole.

Camel memories

I am asked often about the camels,
the trip across the desert,
about going without.

But we had all we needed;
love was our food and shelter,

and years later, when Ted grew stern,
serious,
even hateful,
I'd remind him of our desert time,
laugh at what those camels did.
Their names made me smile,
Mulga, Alice, Burnie, Flossie, Rarji...

and slowly
they would bring him round.

I remember

June 1946

I remember
one night
when Ted was away
and the children
were small and sleeping;
it was summer
and the evening air was cool and soft.

I turned the lights off
and the radio to low,
so as not to wake them,
or their grandparents,

and I danced alone
in the silky dark.

Traces

When will I look up
and think only of me
– of my children.

Wake in the morning
not dreaming of the desert,

when does the red
stop falling from
the pockets and hems
of my clothes,

when does it
finally wash from my body?

Singing

When he comes home,
we gather the family,
him on the piano,
me singing.

My voice always
a true sound in my ears,
a given,

years ago
the singing examiner said I could go a
long way.

Ted's letter

Saturday 21st May 1955

Dear Bertha,
I stood in the doorway of the shack
looking west at Mt Gillen
the sun was setting and
lighting up the broken clouds for the last time today
behind me I could hear you singing,
even though you were far away in Prospect.

It was a sad song,
as though voices from Scotland, Adelaide
and Mt Gillen were all mingling together
expressing the mood of the dying sun,
as yet another day passes into oblivion
and dark eternity.

Wherever I go, it seems
I see only strangers.

What my father wanted

What does any father want for his only daughter?
A good husband, a home, many children,
laughter,
faith and sharing,
a life full of family and grandchildren,
and to grow old with her husband.

He shook my husband's hand at the wedding
said in his kind voice:
'Take care of my girl.'

He didn't see the end,
when love drifted
and the years unfolded sadness.

The truth

The stars tell us so little,
yet I gaze ever hopeful
for some clue,

I pull sounds
from your words –
but there is nothing,
just the space between
holding some unknown
truth to climb into.

Separation

I can barely move
the shame hurts
and the light burns,
like the heat of the desert sun
I had to shield from.

He shames me, has shamed me.
I cry alone,
and hold a smile in place
on the streets.

Horseshoe Bend

I learn from a friend,
Ted has written an account of
his father's death –
finally.

In my kinder moments,
I am glad for him.
Putting ghosts to rest
as it were,
but my harshness surfaces
and I know he cried to *her* about it.

But we all went there
in the end.
All of us in love with
his sad words.
The story of a dying father,
by the dry riverbed
that led to hell.

And we, the women in his life,
cared for him,
listened,
and loved him
like his mother.

3rd October 1978

As the light dims on me
I think of him still,
years try to lessen pain,
the love.

I draw the curtains,
straighten
the tidy room,

but the shadow he cast was long indeed
with me, it seems, always in that shadow.

He dies today,
even that
is a media event.

The gramophone II

I
In the 'good' room I no longer use,
on its own table
is the gramophone.
It came with me
through dust storms lasting days,
that blackened out the sun.

I went gladly with my eyes open
into a marriage with a man of dreams.
Into loss,
four babies lost to the desert,
three who stayed.

I saw my life as a circle,
taking in the country,
like I could see it from the air
long before I flew:
far above the dust
where delicate patterns weave through red sand.
I knew the shape of the desert,
and I could picture where he went
when I could no longer travel with him.

In my mind I trailed behind him,
he, always one step ahead.

I prayed our children, the adventure
would hold him to me,
but his dream took in more than desert.

II
My son and his wife are playing the gramophone,
I hear them laughing
as the music scratches the past.

I am frozen at the doorway
as songs of Central Australia
fill the room,
pulled back in time
when I thought his love
and God's love was all that was needed.

When the tent and the dust
and frozen water
in the washbasin in the mornings
were still part of that love.

When dense mist
hid the mountains and valleys
in mornings
so thick
I thought I could have been
back in the hills
at my father's house.

III
I ask them to stop.
It is only when they turn the music off
that I move from the door
and take my cold tears outside
into the sunlight.

When it comes, the Landscape listens –
Shadows – hold their breath –
When it goes 'tis like the Distance
On the look of Death –
Emily Dickinson

Chronology of events

1911   Bertha Strehlow nee James born in Adelaide 16 April to
Rosamond Delilah Murdoch and George Pugh James of
17 Te Anau Ave, Prospect, South Australia.

1919   Bertha's mother dies from the effects of influenza while
pregnant.
Bertha's father marries Edith Mary Eaton.

1922   Carl Strehlow dies at Horseshoe Bend Station on the Finke
River, 51 years old. Ted is 14 years of age.

1931   Bertha is Head Prefect in her final year at St Peter's Girls
School, Adelaide.

1932   Bertha commences a Bachelor of Arts at the University of
Adelaide.
Ted graduates with Honours in English Literature and
classics, travels to Central Australia for research.

1933   Bertha and Ted meet at the University of Adelaide and soon
after start dating.

1934   Bertha awarded BA in History and Latin from University of
Adelaide.
Bertha starts teaching at Walford Girls School Adelaide.

1935   Ted receives a fellowship from the Australian National
Research Council (ANRC) to investigate the maltreatment of
Aboriginal people in Central Australia.
Bertha and Ted marry 21 December at Prospect, South
Australia.

1936   18 February – arrive in Alice Springs on the Ghan train and
        travel out to Hermannsburg Mission. They stay with Pastor
        and Minna Albrecht and start preparations for the camel trek.
        May – Ted is appointed Patrol Officer for the Central
        Australian region.
        5 June – Bertha and Ted leave Hermannsburg with three
        Aboriginal men, their camel handlers – George, Witchetty
        and Tom Ljonga – and eleven camels for a 1400 mile (2250
        km) camel trek to the Petermann Ranges.
        19 July – in Charlotte Waters, SA. Bertha is unwell and tells
        Ted she is pregnant.
        28 August to 7 September – at Piltadi in the Petermann
        Ranges, Bertha becomes gravely ill following the
        miscarriage.
        25 September – arrive back in Hermannsburg.
        November – Ted and Bertha move to Jay Creek and live in a
        tent.
        December – Christmas visit from Bertha's parents.

1937   29 May – Bertha miscarries a boy.
        22 July – Jay Creek (formally 'The Bungalow') gazetted as the
        Jay Creek Native Reserve.

1938   Bertha miscarries again.
        Ted and three Aboriginal friends make two thousand bricks
        for Ted and Bertha's house, they move into the house in
        mid-1938.
        Albert Namatjira's Exhibition sells out in Melbourne.
        Ted is awarded a Master of Arts for his thesis 'Aranda
        Phonetics and Grammar'.
        Blind Moses, an Aranda evangelist from Hermannsburg,
        becomes the pastor at the Jay Creek Lutheran Church.
        A young Aboriginal woman sick with tuberculosis, Maggie
        Taylor, moves to Jay Creek. Maggie lives in a tent near Bertha
        and Ted and when she recovers she helps Bertha with the
        housework.

1939   Bertha miscarries a fourth time.
        Outbreak of World War II.
        Ted travels to the Petermann Ranges with Pastor Albrecht,
        Dr Charles Duguid and Tom Ljonga, they visit Lasseter's
        Grave near Docker River on the WA/NT border.

1940   Bertha publishes 'Through Central Australia' in *Walkabout,*
        August 1st 1940.
        Ted is accused of being a Nazi by MLA AM Blain in the
        Australian Parliament.
        Jay Creek Lutheran Church official opening on 7 December
        1940.

1942   May – birth of Bertha's first son Theo in Alice Springs.
        Ted released from his Patrol Officer position for military
        service.
        Bertha leaves Central Australia with Theo for her father's
        place in Prospect, Adelaide.

1943   Baby Theo sick with polio, Bertha takes him to Melbourne for
        treatment.

1944   Daughter Shirley is born.

1945   Bertha publishes 'A Camel trip to the Petermann Ranges
        across Central Australia' in *Royal Geographical Society of
        Australasia.*
        22 May – Bertha speaks on local radio about her time in
        Central Australia.
        10 June– Bertha talks on 'Life on an Aboriginal Reserve' to
        the Fellowship of Women Graduates.
        Ted appointed as a lieutenant, based in Canberra at
        Duntroon.
        Second World War ends.

1946   Birth of third child – John.
        Ted commences lecturing in English and Linguistics at
        University of Adelaide.

1946   Bertha starts teaching at Walford School.

1949   Bertha publishes the paper 'Glimpses of Lubra Life' in *Aborigines Friends Association Newsletter.*

1950–2 Ted in England and Europe on a study tour. He visits his mother, Frieda, and his siblings in Germany.

1950   Bertha rents out a room in the house to a boarder, Mr. Lindsay.

1951   February – Bertha starts teaching at Wilderness School. May – a new boarder, Mrs. Morgan, moves into the house with Bertha and her father and children. November – Bertha becomes Vice President of the Women Graduates (Tatlers).

1955   Bertha attends the Conference of the Australian Federation of University Women in Queensland.

1956   Bertha serves as President of the Women Graduates.

1956   Ted completes translation of the New Testament into Aranda.

1957   Frieda Strehlow dies in Germany aged 82 years.

1962   19 August – Bertha's father George James dies in his sleep at Te Anau Ave, aged 84 years.

1967   Bertha travels to Thailand to see her son Theo and his wife Roti.

1968   Bertha attends conference of the International Federation of University Women, in Karlsruhe, Germany. She visits Ted's siblings. Visits daughter Shirley in England for the birth of her first baby. Ted leaves Bertha and moves in with his secretary and research assistant Kathleen Stuart.

1969   Ted publishes *Journey to Horseshoe Bend*.

1971   Ted publishes *Song of Central Australia* (A&U), the writing of which started in the late 1940s.

1972   Bertha divorces Ted on the grounds of desertion. Dame Roma Mitchell presided over the case.
25 September – Ted marries Kathleen. Bertha and her children are disinherited.

1973   Ted and Kathleen have a son – Carl.

1978   3 October – Ted dies at the opening of the Strehlow Research Foundation at the University of Adelaide aged 71.

1983–4   Bertha travels to UK to visit her youngest son John.

1984   30 June – Bertha dies in hospital following a heart attack aged 73.

1985   An agreement is reached between Kathleen Strehlow and Barry Coulter, a MP of the Government of the Northern Territory, on the amount for the purchase of the Strehlow Collection. Plans begin on the construction of the Strehlow Research Centre in Alice Springs.

Map of Bertha's journey

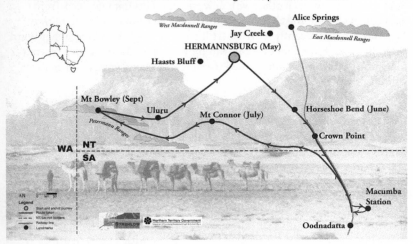

Bertha Strehlow and the Petermann Ranges Expedition of 1936

Map courtesy of the Strehlow Research Centre, Alice Springs

Notes

At the dance Bertha first met Ted Strehlow in 1932 when he was in his Honours year, but it was at a University of Adelaide hockey team dance in 1934 that they saw each other with new eyes. He was not long back from a field trip in Central Australia when he learnt that a young woman he was interested in had recently married (Hill 2003, p. 228). Ted's biographer Ward McNally says, 'From that evening, Strehlow courted Bertha with a fervour that surprised friends, and seemed to sweep the young woman off her feet' (1981, p. 43).

Heart of darkness Bertha's marriage to the brilliant but self-absorbed Ted didn't sit well with many of her friends and throughout her marriage she worked hard to stay in touch with her university friends. She spent a great deal of time smoothing over difficulties between her husband and her family and friends, and often his colleagues (Strehlow, J 2004).

Maps From the start Bertha was struck by the work Ted was doing in Central Australia. She said: 'I was fascinated. I learnt from Ted's diaries the hardships he had often had to endure to perform his work. I began to see him...as a man of courage and compassion, with a great depth of understanding of, and love for, his Aboriginal friends' (quoted in Hill 2003, p. 230). Bertha's unswerving commitment to Ted and his work made it possible for him to carry out his research in Central Australia for extended periods of time (Crawley 1986).

Adelaide Bertha and Ted were married in December 1935 following a whirlwind courtship and a relationship often carried out at long distances. Bertha worked as an English teacher at a girls' school in Adelaide until the wedding and Ted had been in Central Australia on a research trip, so their plans, both for the wedding and for their new life together in Central Australia, were made in the many letters they wrote back and forth to each other in the months prior to the wedding (Strehlow, B 1935, Letters to Ted, Strehlow Research Centre). Three weeks after their wedding they were on a train travelling to Central Australia.

Counselling Bertha was from a well-established Anglican family and, although not wealthy, they were part of the Adelaide establishment. Ted, being from a German Lutheran missionary background, was not seen as a suitable match for Bertha (Strehlow, J 2004, p. 3). Bertha and Ted's youngest son, John Strehlow, has written extensively on the complications and contradictions of his parent's marriage – particularly the ideological differences in their conflicting backgrounds which arose in their relationship in regard to their social, economic and theological attitudes (Strehlow, J 2004 & 2011). Indeed, it was these differences Ted used against Bertha in 1968 when he was justifying his desertion of her. He implied that '...his German and Lutheran background was...completely irksome to her' (in Hill 2003, p. 660).

The train In 1936 the train journey from Adelaide to Alice Springs took two days. Bertha and Ted were travelling in the height of summer and Bertha found the journey unpleasant: 'It was hot and sticky and nearing Alice Springs the train ran into a massive dust-storm. I never believed until then that such climatic conditions existed in Australia...I soaked some hand towels and poked them into the window frames to keep out the dust, but it was useless' (McNally 1981, p. 44). The drought in Central Australia throughout the 1920s and 1930s created massive dust storms across the area (Powell 2009, p. 131; Canberra Times article 24 September 1930). Despite the discomfort, Bertha's attitude remained positive and she displayed intense interest in the world around her.

Alice Springs When Bertha arrived in Alice Springs there were fewer than 900 white people living there. Aboriginal people weren't allowed to stay in the town and were kept at the Telegraph Station 10 kilometres to the north (Powell 2009, p. 129). Bertha and Ted met the nursing sisters at the Australian Inland Mission hostel and they stayed with friends of Ted's to get provisions, before the four-hour drive to Hermannsburg Mission, 120 kilometres west of Alice Springs (McNally 1981, p. 44; Strehlow, B 1955 letter to Ted 24 September; Strehlow TGH 1936 Field Diary XI). The activities of the anthropologist Olive Pink had antagonised Ted for years, since they first met in 1932 at the Australian and New Zealand Association for the Advancement of Science Conference (ANZAAS) where she openly criticised the Aboriginal converts at Hermannsburg mission, saying they were stealing sacred tjuringa [sacred stones] to sell to the missionaries (Markus 2005, p. 65).

To Father from Hermannsburg Bertha was a prolific letter writer and communicated with her father in Adelaide regularly (Bertha Strehlow file,

Strehlow Research Centre). Pastor Albrecht and his wife Minna welcomed Bertha and Ted to Hermannsburg, and provided them with a place to live, as well as two Aboriginal women to help Bertha in the house (Strehlow TGH 1936). The many references to shootings of Aboriginal people by police and settlers caused Ted a great deal of concern and he was pleased to be able to apply for the position of Patrol Officer when it was created in early 1936. At the time he wrote: 'I should be very glad indeed if I could get a position which would enable me to put my life at the service of the interests of the natives of my old home' (ibid.). Despite differences in their upbringings, the importance of Christian service to others was a common belief for them both and Bertha supported Ted's desire to stay and work in Central Australia.

Panic The journey to Central Australia was Bertha's first major journey away from Prospect in Adelaide, and although she was faced with many new situations, she wrote about them as 'a great adventure' (Strehlow, B 1945, p. 9). Living in Hermannsburg, Bertha was experiencing one of the oldest white settlements in Central Australia. It had been established in June 1877 on the banks of the Finke River, west of Alice Springs. The buildings were initially constructed from local timber and thatch, and over time tin was added to the roof and walls (Harris 1990, p. 390). When Bertha arrived the country was still suffering the effects of a long drought and being mid summer it was extremely hot. The buildings had stone floors and the thick stone walls as protection against the heat. But they were not comfortable, as noted many years earlier by Bertha's mother-in-law Frieda Strehlow: 'the rooms were very hot in summer...because the cool night air could not blow through' (Strehlow, J 2011, p. 543).

Heat The early years of the marriage appear to have been very happy and content. A passage described in Hill (2003), reveals the happiness experienced during their time in Hermannsburg: 'They went walking along the Finke, one day going as far as the bend it takes towards Palm Valley, and on another glorious day they strolled upstream...' (ibid., p. 238). There was genuine companionship and a sense of adventure expressed in their writings of this time (Strehlow, B 1945; Strehlow TGH 1936, p. 40).

Trek Bertha was able to place her trust in Ted's abilities as a competent bushman. She writes in a paper published many years after the trek, 'Months before coming to Central Australia, I knew that once here I should spend a year either touring with my husband with the camel team or living in a tent' (1940, p. 9). Ted was very familiar with the country as he had spent many months in Central Australia in 1932, 1933–34 and again in 1935, completing his anthropological research. He travelled over 7000 miles [11265 kilometers] by camel, often only in the company of his long time Aboriginal friend and camel handler Tom Ljonga (Hill 2003, pp. 145–53; Henson 1992, p. 75).

Camels While preparing for the trek at Hermannsburg, Bertha is exposed to camels for the first time. She says of that experience, 'Burney, my husband's lead camel, was the first of the team to be introduced to me, and…I imagined that we should become friends at first sight. However, Burney groaned so horribly when I offered to stroke his head that I was unmoved by any emotion except fear' (Strehlow, B 1940, p. 9).

Photographs Unlike the commonly held belief that '…the "full-bloods" were expected to become extinct through the operation of "natural" evolutionary forces…'(Haebich 2001, p. 18), the work Ted was involved in as a Patrol Officer demonstrated he was opposed to this view. His belief in the role and importance of Aboriginal people in the development of Australia reflects that of his parents who were missionaries at Hermannsburg for 22 years. Bertha was exposed to these policies, and she was critical of the racist and colonial views of the period that assumed the demise of Aboriginal people (Strehlow, B 1945, p. 47).

Music Ted's missionary father, Carl Strehlow, bought an organ in 1896 for his wife Frieda. It is this organ that Ted learnt to play on as a child at Hermannsburg (Henson 1992, p. 75). Bertha sees her husband in a different light being back in the place of his birth where he could recall aspects of his childhood by sharing his love of music that started with the old organ. Bertha herself was a skilled soprano and appeared in recitals in the Adelaide Town Hall while she was still at university. As a couple, they had a mutual love of music and Ted would often accompany Bertha as she sang (Strehlow, J 2004, p. 4; Wall, B 2008 p. 1). Bertha's daughter writes of her mother's love of music, 'As Bertha grew older she declined invitations to sing publicly but began to learn the recorder, and…joined a small recorder group' (Crawley 1986, p. 37).

The gramophone Drawn together by music and the strange wonder of their life together in the desert, Bertha and Ted would dance together in the privacy of the tent they lived in for a time at Hermannsburg after they had to move out of the mission house. 'They also during the 30s liked the blues and used to dance to records from their collection while in the tent…' (Hill 2003, p. 230). Music served as a reflection for Bertha as she acknowledged her new life with Ted in Central Australia.

Camel boxes In 1940, Bertha wrote about the first part of the trek from Hermannsburg to Macumba Station in South Australia. Anticipating the trek to take seven to ten weeks, the camel boxes made by Ted were to contain all the food they needed. Bertha said, '...that meant taking along large supplies of flour, tea, sugar, meat and tinned foods and we had to try and remember all our requirements, because there would be no opportunity to buy extras from the station properties as we went along' (Strehlow, B 1945, pp. 31–2). The quote '...to me through the open window...' is from 'Through Central Australia' (Strehlow, B 1940, p. 9).

Gone There were frustrating delays for Bertha and Ted in getting away from Hermannsburg in the winter of 1936 because they were waiting for more camels to arrive from Alice Springs. Ted wrote that he had hoped to leave in June and said in his diary: 'We have overstayed our welcome [at Hermannsburg], my wife cried in bed last night. She is weary and so am I' (Field diary II 1936–37, p. 10). They finally departed from Hermannsburg on 5 June 1936 and travelled along the Finke River south towards a place called Irbmangkara [Running Waters], an area of the country Bertha found entrancing (Strehlow, B 1945, p. 32).

The eye of a needle Bertha wrote a great deal about the camels she travelled with and, as she got to know them, wrote with increasing affection. '...a fine string through the trees' is from her article 'Through Central Australia' (1940, p. 10). Cars and trucks were being used to explore Central Australia by 1936 but camels were still used to get into more inaccessible country (Barker 1995, p. 129).

Rain The rain and cold weather impacted significantly on the party as they were exposed to the elements daily. Both Ted and Bertha discuss this regularly throughout their writings (Strehlow, TGH 1936 Field Diary 26 July, p. 21). Bertha writes in a letter to her mother-in-law, 'The very first night it rained and I had to attend to things at the fire with a bag over my head, while Ted and the boys covered up the camel boxes with the big tent so that they were protected and we had a shelter' (1936, p. 1). From early in the journey, Bertha helped with the cooking while Ted and their three Aboriginal camel handlers – George, Tom Ljonga and Witchetty – cared for the eleven camels.

Poetry reading The journey initially took them through remarkable country. Bertha writes: 'Here and there, we passed beautiful waterholes, crossed running streams over stepping stones, and once came upon an amphitheatre studded with trees and overhung by giant rock walls, making a retreat as lovely as a walled in garden' (1940, p. 11). At night they read poetry to each other, one of these was Ted's favourite poem: 'The Hollow Men' (Eliot 1954, pp. 67–9).

The silence At the turn of the 19th century and into the early decades of the 20th century, Central Australia was seen as the last frontier, ripe for exploitation by pastoralists and miners. There was intense wrangling between anthropologists, explorers, missionaries and governments around the management of Aboriginal people as their lives were impacted on by the 'development' of the Centre (Powell 2009). This poem, then, is a reflection for Bertha who is experiencing the complexities of Central Australia for the first time in a very exposed way by travelling through the country.

Hoppity In Hermannsburg Ted gave Bertha a joey as a pet and they took it with them on the trek. It proved to be a nuisance, running under the camel's legs, making them shy. They ended up leaving the joey at Horseshoe Bend station (Hill 2003, p. 239). According to Bertha's son John, Ted loved the joey and would get upset whenever it ran away from him to get back to Bertha (J Strehlow pers. comm. 26 June 2013).

The ghosts at Horseshoe Bend The area near Horseshoe Bend on the Finke River has great spiritual significance to the Aranda people and Bertha wrote of this briefly in her 1945 article. At Horseshoe Bend Station she also focused on the immediate topic of the weather which had a daily impact on them: 'It was difficult to make headway against the force of the wind, and clouds gathered overhead, obscuring the sun' (1945, p. 33). The challenging aspects of the bleak weather on the trek was doubly felt because of the events surrounding the death at the same location of Ted's father Carl Strehlow 14 years earlier in 1922, when Ted was just 14 years old (Strehlow, TGH 1969).

Alone with the language Bertha was the only woman on the trek and experienced an extreme sense of isolation, a contrast to her time at Hermannsburg where, even though she didn't speak Aranda or German, she was around women every day. The lack of language could be overcome by the daily domestic routines of the mission and the household, but on the trek she only had Ted to talk to. In letters to her father and stepmother, she writes of enjoying the company of various station women who made her welcome and showed her great kindness (Strehlow, B 1936). She wrote of the companionship she experienced when she and Ted visited Charlotte Waters [324 kilometres south of Hermannsburg]: 'When I first saw it I thought it was the most desolate place I had ever set eyes on. But, after a few hours, I realised the people there really cared for each other more than I believed possible' (McNally 1981, p. 47). Bertha found she was pregnant very early in the camel trek and was ill with morning sickness. There is no record of her talking to anyone about it.

Morning sick When Bertha found she was pregnant, it caused both her and Ted concern instead of joy. Despite the fact that Bertha did not refer to her pregnancy in her writing, Ted wrote extensively about it in his diary. In one entry he wrote, 'My wife and I felt very depressed today. We know now that we can expect an heir in due time if everything goes well. What are we to do? Shall we risk a camel trip for my wife? Her nausea is rather disturbing' (Strehlow, TGH 1936). Throughout the journey Bertha's pregnancy always appeared through Ted's eyes in his diaries.

Patterns The routine of setting up camp was laborious and took several hours each day. When the camp was set up Ted cooked for everyone and distributed food to the Aboriginal men, a routine that controlled and conserved the food supplies. It was a routine that was established at Hermannsburg Mission by Ted's father Carl Strehlow and continued by Pastor FW Albrecht when he took over the management of Hermannsburg Mission in 1926 (Henson 1992, p. 28; Edmond 2013, p. 107).

Ancient light After leaving Lyndavale Station in early August, the party travelled west for 100 kilometres towards Mt Connor, much of the time traversing 10-metre-high sand dunes. They saw the Musgrove Ranges to the south, and the shape of Mt Connor on the horizon before them for many days before they reached it. When recording the slow movement across the country, Bertha often included passages describing the vegetation and landscape (1945, p. 37–8). On her return to Hermannsburg she wrote: '...our progress out to the Reserve was very slow 18 or 20 miles being the best that we could manage on most days' (1936, p. 1).

Late afternoon The party travelled for around six hours each day, with the unpacking and packing up again the next day taking a great deal of time. It was a gruelling schedule that Ted mentioned frequently in his diaries (1936), but Bertha rarely mentioned this in the papers she wrote about the journey, where she focuses on descriptions of the landscape (1940 & 1945).

Rage The physical and emotional support Bertha provided to Ted, which made his work recording Aboriginal stories and legends possible, really began on this journey. Her generous nature gave him the space within the relationship to develop his research (Hill 2003, p. 230).

Mt Connor This is a 'found poem' from Bertha's published essay 'A camel trip to the Petermann Ranges across Central Australia' (Strehlow, B 1945, pp. 39–40). George was one of the Aboriginal guides on the journey. He was a Pitjantjatjara man from the far south-western part of the Northern Territory, and the Mt Connor area (Atila) was on the borders of his traditional country and Bertha and Ted recorded him as being happy to be there again. Layton explains that this feeling is something deeper than being happy to be home; rather it is a cultural experience of coming into country where specific songs and chants need to be sung that are linked to the dreaming stories at the site and the health of the country (1986, pp. 43–4).

Night falls cold Their trek went west towards the South West Native Reserve, to investigate an allegation of the shootings of three Aboriginal men near the Petermann Ranges (Strehlow, TGH 1936, p. 10). Bertha was ill on and off with morning sickness and had experienced some distressing episodes of pain and cramping which resulted in severe bleeding (p. 42).

Speaking country The movement experienced while travelling across country has a rhythm all of its own and being in remote areas can create a sense where time moves at a different pace. For Bertha, this experience was embodied in the movement of the camels and the distances travelled through the landscape (Hill 2001, p. 93).

Inland Sea Bertha wrote extensively about the lack of water and game in the South West Native Reserve and the devastation of the country caused by the drought and the introduction of cattle into Central Australia. She said of the ruined country: 'People wonder why the aborigines refuse to stay in the reserves that they have been granted to them, but are they to be blamed if they wander out of the reserves and live, instead of staying there to die of starvation?' Much of Bertha's record of her journey was dominated by accounts of the degraded condition of the country (1945, p. 47).

Haircutting at Piltadi The trek arrived at Piltadi waterhole for the first time on 24 August 1936. Bertha had been bleeding on and off for a week but in a letter to her mother-in-law she does not mention this. Rather, she speaks of practical things: 'there we sat down for a week to rest ourselves and our camels and do our washing, haircutting and other odd jobs' (Strehlow, B 1936, p. 2). Bertha was probably suffering a 'threatened miscarriage'. The constant travel would have contributed to her increasing ill health but it is difficult to know if she had ceased all travel at this stage if she would have recovered and been able to carry the child to term (Kitzinger 1982, p. 339).

Mt McCulloch Once in the Petermann Ranges, Ted had work to do investigating the disappearance of three young Aboriginal men who had been missing since the reports of a shooting near Mt Bowley in the Petermann Ranges by the expedition searching for Lasseter (Adelaide Advertiser, 2 July 1936; Strehlow TGH, 1936–37 Diary 11, pp. 36–41). Ted reported in his diary, 'Whether the story of the shooting tragedy is true or not, time will tell...' (ibid., p. 35). Ted was juggling the pressure of his work and his concern for Bertha's wellbeing.

Reading the sand Bertha had to stay away from the discussions Ted was having with the Pitjantjatjara men: 'After greeting [the men] in Aranda, Ted was invited to sit and talk. Bertha remained some distance away – as did Tom Ljonga and the trackers: this was 'foreign' country to them' (McNally 1981, p. 51). Meeting these old men was an unexpected bonus as both Bertha and Ted regularly wrote that the South West Native Reserve was empty of people, the devastating results of colonisation impacting on Aboriginal populations through illness, pastoral demands imposing on hunting grounds and massacres. This contrasts to pre-contact days where '...in spite of the wide open spaces, Aboriginal people in the desert were neither alone or subject to random movements, rather there was profound and purposeful movements influenced by the weather and seasons' (Clarke 2003, p. 141; Layton 1986, pp. 45–5).

Kungkarrangkalpa Bertha is likely to have read the story of the Seven Sisters when she edited Ted's work (Strehlow, J 2004; Strehlow TGH 1971). There are many versions of the Seven Sisters creation story among different language groups in the south and west of Central Australia that explains the formation of the 'mythopoetic landscape' of the desert country in the south and west of the Northern Territory (James 2009, p. 13). The many forms of retelling (song, dance and oral) are examples of how when a story is told and retold appropriately to strangers it can become a metaphor for the meeting of cultures. Layton writes: 'Legends are not told in their full form at once: incidents are related when an occasion arises to visit the appropriate place and gradually more profound aspects of the narrative are revealed to give a deeper understanding of why the legends play so central a part in Aboriginal life within the region' (1986 p. 5). For Bertha, this involved writing up the traditional stories told to Ted by a number of Aboriginal men who talked to him over a long period of time (Strehlow, TGH 1936).

Camping east of Mt Philips Ted identified stongly with Central Australia and in particular with the Aranda; indeed, Ted's biographer Hill (2003) wrote that Ted was convinced he was a lone voice speaking up for Aranda people.

In Bertha, he had found an accepting and loving partner who believed in him and what he was doing. Her writings of this time demonstrate her ability to be open minded and accepting of the situations she found herself in, fed by the love she felt for Ted (Strehlow, B 1936, 1940, 1945 & 1949; Hill 2003, p. 230; McNally 1981, pp. 43–4). She was increasingly unwell, but this was a better day for Bertha.

Mt Bowley In a letter to her mother-in-law after the camel trek, Bertha briefly mentions the miscarriage but focuses on the spiritual aspect of the experience rather than the grave physical danger she was in (1936, p. 3). The complications of miscarrying at 12 weeks are haemorrhage and infection if the miscarriage was 'incomplete', and both situations can result in a medical emergency (Kitzinger 1982, pp. 339–40). Bertha was lucky to have survived. She and Ted felt very strongly that she had been spared by an act of God. The mention of Lasseter's grave is like a coded message, acknowledging that her child too was buried nearby (Strehlow, B 1945 p. 44). The 'found poem' is the closest I can find in Bertha's writing to where she hints at her miscarriage and illness.

Nothing As Bertha wrote many letters, it is logical that she wrote to her father in Adelaide of her experiences in the desert. But as always she was intensely private and was unlikely to have revealed the cause of her illness, instead discussing the landscape and the country about her. The poem imagines her external calmness in the form of a letter, a contrast to her internal struggle in the face of possible death. This quiet moment of reflection is expressed by artist Ruark Lewis: '...a poem on the page is like a window' (1999), acknowledging her experiences, enabling her father to develop a picture of the desert.

Beauty Ted recorded the events of the night that they thought could be Bertha's last. They prayed together and he wrote that they made confessions to each other. The couple told each other of their past sins and both felt greatly relieved afterwards, then Bertha's cramping subsided somewhat (Strehlow TGH 1936, p. 46). Hill writes, 'It was in this state of naked dependence...' that they felt a new level of closeness with each other (2003, p. 243). Their Aboriginal helpers had gone east towards Mt Olga in search of water, their food supplies were very low and their situation is looking grim. Ted wrote, 'She is reading our bible now' (p. 46).

At the waterhole The threat of death for Bertha was very real because of the extreme remoteness of their location and because there was no option of being rescued. Even if they had taken a radio, there was no facilities available to bring Bertha back to Alice Springs. The statistics reveal that the rate of maternal deaths in the Northern Territory did not decline until after 1920 and even then remained twice as high as for the rest of the country.

If I speak from under the earth The country opened up to Bertha and she could 'see' it as if for the first time. The experience at Piltadi had taken her into new depth of understanding of herself and the country she was in. The concept of understanding the country from the 'inside' is expressed by Anna Couani: 'The map of the world is felt from the inside.../Reading with the fingers as though blind. Feeling it with the back, down the spine.../ Flying low but fast across the land masses' (Hampton & Llewellyn 1986, p. 198). Bertha's experience was mirrored in the idea that she could see that Indigenous lands are 'saturated with meaning' (San Roque, Dowd & Tacey, 2011, p. 126).

The women The accounts of the Aboriginal women who assisted Bertha are documented by Wall (2008) and McNally (1981, p. 63). Neither Bertha nor Ted mentions this moment in their writings. The herb given to Bertha in a tea infusion was mostly likely the native desert shrub Eremophila longifolia which is found across Central Australia (Latz 1995, pp. 176–7). Called 'tulypurpa' in Pitjantjatjara, it is given to women following childbirth to help stop bleeding (Goddard 1992, p. 223). Before white people arrived in Central Australia the herb was administered by passing 'smoking' branches over the woman, but after the arrival of white people Aboriginal people used billies to boil water and this herb was made into an infusion and given as a drink (Latz 1995).

Skies and waterholes Years after she'd left central Australia, Bertha wrote: 'On a trip I once took with my husband across the South-west Native Reserve we met a few natives near Mount Olga who could still be described as entirely primitive in their way of life.' These could be the women who brought her herbs, as this is the area near where she miscarried. In an account by Wall (2008, p. 3) who wrote a biographical piece on Bertha, it says: 'They were in the outback, miles from anywhere. He [Ted] fashioned a...stretcher on his camel's near side, lifted Bertha into it...and led the camel in the direction where he might find aboriginal help. The group he met was unknown to him but they understood his Aranda language, trusted him and were willing to help. The aboriginal women knew what to do and Bertha's life was saved.' Their knowledge was the link between life and death for Bertha, but the reality of how close they came to another outcome haunted Bertha and Ted every step back to Hermannsburg.

Flossie Bertha wrote: 'The problem immediately arose of how we were to get home as I couldn't possibly ride a camel and we couldn't stay there indefinitely...Ted cut down 2 forked mulga branches and tied 3 long straight poles to them to form the seat and back. Then he covered these with hessian and put a board at the back for the headrest. It was strapped to the side of the camel like an ordinary load and an equal load was filled into the pack bags and hung on the other side...' (1936, p. 3). Bertha was carried for the 300 miles [482 kilometres] to Hermannsburg Mission.

The Olgas Bertha was very weak as the party travelled towards Mt Olga (1936, p. 3), but she gives nothing away: 'Mt Olga lay sixty miles from Piltadi, and we could see it for most of the way. It appeared as a blue shadow on the horizon at first – a shadow with many domes. As we drew closer the colour changed to rose pink and then to dark red, and the rocky mass appeared to form a cluster of gigantic boulders heaped together' (1945, p. 45).

The first white woman Bertha had seen Ayers Rock from a distance a month earlier as she and Ted had travelled west towards the Petermanns; now she was coming into its folds. Many years later she wrote: 'We found a quality of water on the southern side of the rock, and replenished our supplies at a pool which was icy cold because the sun's rays could not reach over the high rock wall' (1945, p. 46). At Ayers Rock the party could spend time at a reliable water source before the waterless journey of 190 miles north towards Palm Valley (1936, p. 4). Many parties of white explorers had passed by the Rock since Gosse had first recorded seeing it in his diary on 19 July 1873 (1973). All of the white travellers prior to Bertha were men.

Sound It is not without significance that Bertha spent some her time recovering at the base of Uluru at Maggie Springs. This waterhole – now referred to by its Pitjantjatjara name, Kupi Mutitjulu – is a sacred women's place of healing and creation. It is part of the 'ground journeys of the seven sisters' (Isaacs 1984, p. 241). These are formation stories explaining the creation of the landscape, with different versions told to women and men, and others to strangers. For Bertha, this place was one of restoration and safety. The Rock curves around the waterhole like protective arms. It is reverent and the quiet is profound (Strehlow 1945, p. 46).

Dear mother Found poem taken from a letter Bertha wrote to her mother-in-law Frieda Strehlow in Germany after she and Ted arrived back in Hermannsburg on 25 September 1936. She wrote: 'I am quite well and have been since about a fortnight after the event. Neither of us regrets it...' She wrote with warmth and was positive throughout the letter as she focused on the spiritual experience they had and played down the life-threatening experience she had faced in the desert (1936, p. 4).

The tent Bertha and Ted lived in a tent for two years at Jay Creek while they waited for their house to be built, they called it 'their island'. Tired of waiting, Ted started making the bricks himself with help from Aboriginal workers (Hill 2003, p. 322). Biographers Barbara Wall and Ward McNally cite Bertha's fear of snakes. There was good reason, as Ted wrote in an entry in his journal: 'More snake tracks were visible in our tent this morning' (Strehlow, TGH 1936).

Journals In 1991, 50 years after Bertha's time in Central Australia, the Strehlow Research Centre was opened in Alice Springs. It was a purpose-built facility to house the 15 kilometres of movie film, 7,000 slides, thousands of pages of genealogical records, audio recordings, letters, 42 field diaries and over 700 sacred objects that Ted had collected over his many years in the field (Hill 2003, p. 20).

Outhouse Bertha's ability to make do meant she coped well with the conditions and situations she found herself in. Ted's biographer writes: 'Bertha quickly showed herself to be a most unexpected type of city-girl cheerfully setting up house under canvas..."it was adventurous, and for most of the time she enjoyed it"' (McNally 1981, p. 56).

The horses at Jay Creek Feral horses were introduced into Central Australia with the arrival of white settlers and explorers but weren't as well suited as camels in the desert landscape. They were used predominately in the cattle industry for the mustering and movement of cattle, but many escaped and over time adapted to the desert conditions (Barker 1995, p. 129). They roamed the Jay Creek Native Reserve, visiting waterholes at dusk.

Dream language The 20th century explorer Ernest Giles gave the Petermann Ranges their non-Indigenous name. Bertha's dream state is explored by investigating the parallels in this imagined dream of Bertha's with Giles' writing: 'Darkness began to creep over this solitary place...I coiled myself up under a bush and fell into one of those extraordinary waking dreams which occasionally descend upon imaginative mortals when we know that we are alive, and yet we think we are dead...At such a time the imagination can revel only in the marvelous, (sic) the mysterious, and the mythical' (Carter 1987, pp. 84–5).

Burning Ted was frustrated that his recommendations for a food/ration depot in the South West Native Reserve to be established to prevent starvation among the Pitjantjatjara people and to stop them from leaving the area were ignored. He wrote: 'The southern part, viz the Petermann Ranges is rapidly approaching the same degree of desolation [as in 1936]. In the report I furnished three years ago the danger of such an evacuation of the Reserve was pointed out, and the establishment of a ration depot suggested as an immediate remedy to relieve the situation' (Strehlow TGH 1941, pp. 15–8). Bertha spent much of her time, in this instance and on many other occasions, calming Ted and helping him to tone down his responses to the government officials (Strehlow, J 2004).

113° F Drought conditions were part of a long-term weather pattern recorded by white explorers as 1890–91, 1915–17, 1931–39 (Layton 1986, p. 34), and in later years drought was seen as more of a norm. As described by Latz: 'On the whole, drought years are more frequent than exceptionally good years' (1995, p. 3). In 1941 Ted was supplied with a car to assist with his travel in the area and Bertha would often accompany him on these trips (VJ White, 17 April 1941).

Fire Aboriginal people used fire to hunt and to regenerate plant life. Although this practice continued to some extent in Bertha's time, traditional land-management practices were not understood by white settlers. Thus administrators exercised control over the lives of Aboriginal people but also over the environment. Jay Creek ran herds of goats as a way of creating employment for the Aboriginal residents and as a form of income for the settlement (Hill 2003, p. 304).

Small things Bertha had a further three miscarriages after her trek across the desert. Each time she was extremely ill. Reference to a car passing by on the way to Stanley Chasm on 13 June 1937, following Bertha's second miscarriage on Saturday 29 May, is found in Ted's diaries (1937). Ted regularly recorded Bertha's physical condition: 'Dr. Riley visited [from Alice Springs] in Don Thomas' car'. On 11 June, Bertha 'walked around the camp' and 'sat up for 6 hours'. On another day Ted writes that Bertha 'sat in the garden and had her first meal' and 'a car passed by on the way to Stanley Chasm' (TGH Strehlow 1937 Personal diary No. 3, SRC). The loss of a child, especially a miscarriage, was difficult to talk about without fault being levelled at the woman, as was implied by Bertha herself in her letter to her mother-in-law (1936). This poem reflects a tradition of eulogy in poetry as explored by poet Deb Westbury: '...a name he didn't expect,/even then,/ to live all the way into' (2002, p. 63). Bertha appears not to have spoken or written about her ill health from her debilitating miscarriages, nor of the impact this would have had on her marriage.

Songs of Central Australia Sharing a title with TGH Strehlow's major work Songs of Central Australia published in 1971 (Allen & Unwin), this poem acknowledges the typing and editing which Bertha did over the six years of living in Jay Creek Native Reserve and also in the years that followed in Adelaide. Much of the early editing of this book occurred while she lived in the tent at Jay Creek and she was never acknowledged for this work. It was a small community and there was tight control over the lives of the Aboriginal and non-Aboriginal people who lived at Jay Creek where everyone knew everyone else's business (NT Administration Report, 1937, p. 25).

Walking east I have imagined that Bertha had an understanding of hand signs, which are a distinct form of communicating in Central Australia. Sign languages were in daily use in Arandic communities of Central Australia as an extension of the spoken language (Green et al. 2011). Much of the country around Jay Creek is sacred and out of bounds to women, and Bertha would have had knowledge of this from her editing of Ted's work (Strehlow, TJ 2006, p. 1).

To Hermann Vogelsang Bertha typed up all Ted's letters and this poem refers to the letter Ted wrote to Hermann Vogelsang, who was looking for work as an overseer at the newly established Jay Creek. His father had been a lay missionary at Coopers Creek in the early 1870s working with the Dieri and was known to Carl Strehlow. The Dieri were the people of the Coopers Creek area who helped John King, the surviving member of the 1862 Burke and Wills expedition. Their generosity to the expedition created a great deal of interest in them and led to settlers and missionaries moving into the area up until the end of the 19th century. Their population was decimated by this contact and by 1915 the Lutheran mission at Bethesda was closed because the numbers of Dieri had dwindled so dramatically. In the 1890s the New Testament was translated into Dieri by Carl Strehlow and J Reuther (Harris 1990, pp. 385–9; Strehlow, J 2011, pp. 308–15).

Language lessons There are no accounts of Bertha being able to speak Aranda; in fact her son John, in his writings, is critical of her not being able to speak more than a few words of Aranda despite her living at Jay Creek for six years (Strehlow, J 2004). The spelling of 'Aranda' is consistent with the spelling at the time Bertha was living in Central Australia. It is now spelt 'Arrernte' but it was also spelt 'Aranta', 'Arunta' and 'Arunda' in different texts (Turpin 2004; Edmond 2013).

Maggie In August 1938 a young Aboriginal woman called Maggie Taylor was sent to Jay Creek from the 'Half-Caste Institution' in Alice Springs because she had been diagnosed with tuberculosis of the larynx. She camped near

Ted and Bertha's tent rather than with the other Aboriginal families to avoid infecting others with TB. Requests for more provisions for Maggie were denied (TGH field diary 1937). Bertha typed up many letters for Ted about Maggie; these were sent to the Chief Protector of Aborigines, CEA Cook, but to no avail (Strehlow, TGH 1938). After being cared for by Bertha, Maggie became well again and helped Bertha in the house for a time before being sent back to the Half-Caste Institution (ibid.). Maggie became a close friend of Bertha's and returned to Jay Creek to help Bertha during her pregnancy and following the birth of her first child Theo (pers. comm. Olga Radke November 2014, SRC).

Weaving hands Bertha was regularly called on to assist with medical matters at Jay Creek as medical help was 45 kilometres away in Alice Springs (Strehlow, TGH 1941, 7 February Report). It was expected she would work in the community and she was never paid. In a letter to Ted from Mr Chinnery, Director of Native Affairs, dated 25 November 1941, there was a suggestion that Bertha take up the position of Women's Protector. Ted replied: 'As you know, my wife has always had the burden of keeping watch over the natives on the Jay Creek Reserve during my trips to other stations in the Centre; and thus she has given out rations, attended to the sick...' (Strehlow, TGH, 9 December 1941). But Ted makes it clear that Bertha wouldn't be accepting the role.

The birth Maternal mortality rates in remote areas were extremely high for both Indigenous and non-Indigenous women due to blood loss, sepsis and the lack of adequate medical attention. The institutionalisation of Aboriginal people on missions and cattle stations in increasing numbers, following the drought and loss of traditional lands, resulted in a major change in diet from hunting and gathering to one based primarily on flour, sugar and tea, and in the late 1930s maternal deaths from malnutrition were common (Franklin & White 1991, p. 16). Bertha had the onerous task of caring for the ill and there were many deaths during her time at Jay Creek. She told her daughter-in-law years later that she'd thought of herself as the 'white medicine man' at Jay Creek but her medicines were limited to eucalyptus-based preparations for colds and aches and pains (Strehlow, R 2006, p. 2).

First born In late 1941 Bertha was pregnant once again and she must have been wondering by now if she would ever be able to carry a baby to term. On the advice of her doctor, Orme Kewish, she followed a strict regime of bed rest and a special diet for the first six months of her pregnancy. She was determined to make sure this pregnancy went to term (Wall 2008, p. 3;

Strehlow, J 2004, p. 8) Her son John wrote: 'She was only able to have children by going to bed for about 6 months each time, taking special medicine and eating a special diet' (ibid). Bertha remained silent on these matters, not recording any of the details in her writing.

The first crack While living at Jay Creek, Ted travelled widely, on patrol in Central Australia to other Aboriginal communities as well as to Adelaide University and Canberra (Hill 2003). Bertha remained at home in Jay Creek and took on the role of managing the Jay Creek Reserve (Strehlow, TGH 1939 & 1941, 7 February).

At the end of the frost Bertha's pregnancy had gone well and she was about to give birth to their first son Theodor at the hospital in Alice Springs which had expanded during the Second World War. The effects of the war were felt in the desert with Alice Springs becoming 'a major supply base for thousands of Australian and American troops stationed in the north' (Edmond 2013, p. 183). Following the birth of Theo, Ted was called up to the Army and had to leave for Duntroon, in Canberra. Maggie Taylor came and helped Bertha with baby Theo but Bertha knew her time in Central Australia was coming to an end. There were difficulties 'obtaining a home of their own' so Bertha and baby Theo moved into Bertha's old family home in Adelaide with her father. 'At the end of the frost' is a line from Bertha's writing (1945).

Writing distance In 1942 Bertha was living in Adelaide back at her childhood home in Prospect. Despite this, Bertha's energies and thoughts focused on Central Australia for many years to come as Ted's work took him back to the area regularly. Often Bertha was the sole breadwinner, with her wages supporting his research. She continued typing up and editing his work, as well as sourcing film and photographic supplies, and on one occasion sent up boxes of oranges for the Hermannsburg Mission on the train (Letters to Ted 1942–1962).

The dream Central Australia remained an important part of Bertha's life long after she'd left, and she reflected on this often in her many letters (Letters 1945–62). Bertha focused on nature in her writing and this poem imagines her remembering Central Australia when it was in the grip of drought and the opposite to this dream: 'The bush was absolutely silent, as there were no birds even to be seen' (1945, p. 41).

Camel memories Bertha gave a number of talks and presentations on the radio in Adelaide about her time in Central Australia. She wrote to Ted about it when they were apart, saying to him she would rather that he be the one to talk as he was the expert (Letters 22 May 1945, 3 July 1945). She spoke of Ted's work as a way of creating interest and possible funding for his research, but she also spoke about the living conditions of Aboriginal people and the difficulties she felt they faced in a changing world. Some of the camels for the 1936 trek came from the police officer in Alice Springs and were returned after. Others, including Bertha's favourite, Flossie, remained at Hermannsburg and were used again by Ted in his 1939 trek.

I remember Bertha and Ted moved into her father's house in Prospect, South Australia after they left Jay Creek. It was a small three-bedroom house and they often had a boarder living there to help pay the bills. The children Theo (born 1942), Shirley (born 1944) and John (born 1946) grew up in this house, and Bertha wrote frequently to Ted when he was away on research trips in Central Australia, interstate and overseas, keeping him up with family life (various letters from Bertha to Ted 1945–1962). Bertha told Ted's biographer of the many letters she had written to Ted: 'I wanted Ted to be able to slip easily into his place as our head of family, with as full an understanding of the children as possible. I thought that was very important. And anyway our correspondence was a source of joy to me. I think Ted enjoyed it too' (1981, p. 76).

Traces Bertha thought a lot about going back to Central Australia as she wrote in a letter to Ted: 'I have been amusing myself during the last few nights just before I went to sleep pretending that we were both to go up with Theodor...[w]hat a triumphant return for us both to go back with our son' (9th July 1945). This letter holds many echoes of the past: her miscarriages, her ill health and the efforts required to carry a baby to term, but also of the fact that Ted was born in Hermannsburg and that he could bring his own son there. In the end, Bertha returned only once to Central Australia after moving to Adelaide, when she and Ted brought the three children to Hermannsburg in 1949. Their son Theo recalls this as a difficult time with pressure placed on him by Ted to learn Aranda and bush skills during the two months the family was at Hermannsburg (Strehlow TJ 2004, p. 103).

Singing After she returned to live in Adelaide Bertha was sought after to sing at events again (Letter to Ted, 1945). Bertha was a soprano, and had sung in recitals in Adelaide before her marriage (Hill 2003; letter from Bertha to Ted 1933). Later in life her son John taught her the recorder which she played until her death in 1984.

Ted's letter After Bertha and Ted returned to Adelaide in 1942, Ted continued to visit Central Australia on research trips. When apart they were prolific letter writers, sometimes writing to each other twice or more each week. In 1955 when this letter was written, Ted was in Central Australia working with a group of old men from Hermannsburg, recording traditional songs and chants in Aranda. Bertha's letters to him were full of news of the children and social events she'd attended, and Ted's replies were often like this one, full of melancholia and sadness (Bertha's letters to Ted 18–29 May 1955; TGH Strehlow 1955 Field Diary XIX).

What my father wanted Bertha's father adored her and the children. Bertha's daughter writes about him as a quiet and gentle man: 'He was an important influence on all of us, and during the adolescence of my brothers and myself he extended his support of Bertha by accompanying us on several holidays. My father always claimed that he was too busy to go with us' (Crawley 1986, p. 37). Bertha's father George James died in his sleep at home in August 1962 at the age of 84.

The truth Bertha went overseas in 1967 to visit her and Ted's eldest son Theo in Thailand. When she came back Ted had moved into the spare room and by early 1968 he had moved to live with Kathleen Stuart. She was a high school teacher who had moved to Adelaide in 1964 with her author husband Donald Stuart and their two children. Ted had been tutoring her in English Literature at the University of Adelaide and she had started working as his research assistant. Ted and Kathleen lived one street away from Bertha in Prospect (Hill 2003, p. 660).

Separation When Ted left Bertha in 1968, she was working as a teacher and was active in community groups in Adelaide. She was extremely quiet about the separation and told very few people (Wall 2008). Bertha sued for divorce on the grounds of desertion in 1972. 'She did not seek maintenance. She proudly stated that as a senior teacher at Wilderness School for Girls, her salary was ample for her needs' (in Hill 2003 p. 700). Her son John reflects: '...when the judge, Justice Mitchell, the first woman judge in SA, asked her if she wanted a clause included in the settlement about our father's will, she said no, so we were totally disinherited of everything...' (2004, p. 5).

Horseshoe Bend Ted published *Journey to Horseshoe Bend* about the death of his father Carl Strehlow in 1969 (Rigby) using the diary he kept as a 14-year-old boy. Even though the work is memoir, it is written in the third-person narrative, with Ted referring to himself throughout as Theo (Carter 1996). After the death of his father at Horseshoe Bend, Ted and his mother Frieda travelled to Adelaide where they lived until Ted started university. Only then did Frieda travel back to Germany to be reunited with her other five children. Bertha was all too familiar with this tragic story of loss, and Ted was known for his dramatic moods and sadness about his family. Ted had divorced Bertha by the time the book was published (Hill 2003; Strehlow, J 2004).

3rd October 1978 Ted Strehlow died of a heart attack on the day of the opening of the Strehlow Research Foundation at the University of Adelaide. He collapsed in the arms of Justice Michael Kirby who was present to open the Research Foundation (Hill 2003, p. 757). Bertha lived for another six years and died in 1984 following a heart attack. Up until then she was extremely active, volunteering at the Lutheran Mission offices in Adelaide, playing in a recorder group, and regularly attending the opera and theatre with her friends. She had made firm friends with many people in Central Australia and kept in regular contact with them (Strehlow, J 2004). Ted left his life's work and collection to his second wife Kathleen and their only son Carl. Bertha and her children were not acknowledged in his will (Hill 2003).

The gramophone II A short essay by Bertha's long-time friend, Debbie Little, was written for 'The Desert Honeymoon' exhibition held at the Strehlow Research Centre, Alice Springs in June 2006 in honour of Bertha and her achievements and experiences in Central Australia in the 1930s. Little wrote: 'A haunting memory for me was her [Bertha's] appearance in the doorway of a room in which John and I were playing records on an old gramophone...the look on her face was tragic and it was clear from the tears in her eyes that it was a genuinely painful memory for her' (Little 2004, p.2).

References

Adelaide Advertiser, 'Alleged Shooting in Native Reserve', 2 July 1936.

Canberra Times, Wednesday 24 September 1930, 'Drought in Central Australia', http://trove.nla.gov.au/ndp/del/article/2332990.

Commonwealth of Australia, Report on the Administration of the Northern Territory, 30 June, 1936, published 22 June, 1938, p. 25.

Crawley, S, 1986, 'Shirley Crawley writes of her mother, Bertha Strehlow', *Greater than their knowing...A glimpse of South Australian Women 1836-1986*, eds A. Taylor & V. Mignon, Wakefield Press, p. 36.

Gosse, WC & Libraries Board of South Australia, 1973 (1874), *WC Gosse's explorations, 1873: report and diary of Mr. WC Gosse's central and western exploring expedition, 1873*, Adelaide Government Printer, 1874, Libraries Board of South Australia.

James, G, 1936, Letter to TGH Strehlow, 13 July 1936, Strehlow Research Centre, Alice Springs.

Little, D, 2004, 'Memories of Bertha Strehlow', Desert Honeymoon Exhibition, Strehlow Research Centre, Alice Springs.

Radke, O, 2014, Personal Communication, Strehlow Research Centre, Alice Springs, 7 November 2014.

Saddler, P, 'Bertha Strehlow', unpublished epigraph for Tatler's Club, University of Adelaide pp. 1-2.

Strehlow, B, 1945-55, Letters to Ted Strehlow, viewed 21-28 June 2013, Strehlow Research Centre, courtesy of J. Strehlow.

Strehlow, B, 1949, 'Glimpses of Lubra Life in Central Australia,' in *Aborigines Friends Association* Annual Report, p. 33.

Strehlow, B, 1945, 'A Camel trip to the Petermann Ranges across Central Australia', in *Royal Geographical Society of Australasia, Proceedings for the 1944-1945*, Vol. XLVI, December 1945, Gill York Gate Benham Libraries, Adelaide.

Strehlow, B, 1940, 'Through Central Australia', in *Walkabout,* Vol. 6, No. 10, August 1940.

Strehlow, B, 1936. Letter to Frieda Strehlow, unpublished, Strehlow Research Centre, Alice Springs, pp. 14.

Strehlow, B, 1933, Letter to Ted Strehlow, Strehlow Research Centre, Alice Springs.

Strehlow, J, 2013, Personal communication, Alice Springs, 26 June 2013.

Strehlow, J, 2011, *The Tale of Frieda Keysser: Frieda Keysser & Carl Strehlow – an historical biography,* Wild Cat Press, London.

Strehlow, J, 2004, 'About Bertha Strehlow', Strehlow Research Centre, Alice Springs, p. 3.

Strehlow, R, 2006, 'My mother in law', Bertha Strehlow file, Strehlow Research Centre, Alice Springs, p. 2.

Strehlow, TGH, 1971, *Songs of Central Australia,* A&U, Sydney.

Strehlow, TGH, 1969, *Journey to Horseshoe Bend,* Rigby, Melbourne.

Strehlow, TGH, 195,5 Field Diary XIX, Strehlow Research Centre, Alice Springs.

Strehlow, TGH, 1941 Report – TGH Strehlow Patrol Officer Jay Creek 7th February 1941, National Archive of Australia, Darwin Office, CRS F126, Item 37, p. 7 http://www.cifhs.com/ntrecords/ntgeneral/strehlow_37_Jay_Creek.html viewed 3rd September 2014.

Strehlow, TGH, 1938, 'Report re Half-caste Maggie from Mount Cavenagh Station', 2 August 1938, AA CRS F126, Item 27, Strehlow Research Centre, Alice Springs.

Strehlow, TGH, 1937–1942, 'Hermannsburg c. 1934–1937 TGH Strehlow Patrol Officer 1937–1942', AA(NT) F126/36 Reports folder, Strehlow Research Centre, Alice Springs.

Strehlow, TGH, 1937, Personal Diary No. 3, 1937, unpublished, Strehlow Research Centre, Alice Springs.

Strehlow, TGH, 1936, Field Diary XI, 1936–1937, unpublished, Strehlow Research Centre, Alice Springs.

Strehlow, TGH, 1936, Field Diary II B/27 1936–1937, unpublished, Strehlow Research Centre, Alice Springs.

Strehlow, TGH, 1932, Field Diary, unpublished, Strehlow Research Centre, Alice Springs.

Strehlow, TJ, 2006, 'In Memoriam of my mother, Bertha Strehlow', Bertha Strehlow file, Strehlow Research Centre, Alice Springs, p. 1.

Strehlow, TJ, 2004, 'Memories of my Father: TGH Strehlow', *Traditions in the midst of change,* Proceedings of the Strehlow Conference 2002, Strehlow Research Centre, NTG, Alice Springs, p. 103.

Wall, B, 2008, *Native Tongue: A tribute to Bertha Strehlow,* Tatlers Club Newsletter, University of Adelaide, p. 3.

White, VJ, 1941, Letter to TGH Strehlow, 17th April 1941, Strehlow Research Centre, Alice Springs.

Other sources cited

Bardon, G, 2006 (1991), *Papunya Tula Art of the Western Desert,* Gecko Books, Melbourne, p. 78.

Barker, HM, 1995 (1964), *Camels and the Outback,* Hesperian Press, WA, first published Sir Isaac Pitman & Son Ltd, p. 129.

Dickinson, E, (1997), 'No. 449, I died for beauty' & 'No. 258, There's a certain Slant', in *Emily Dickinson,* ed. H. McNeil, Orion Publishing Group, London, pp. 12 & 31.

Edmond, M, 2013, *Battarbee and Namatjira,* Giromondo, Sydney.

Eliot, TS, 1954, 'The Hollow Men', in *Selected Poems,* Faber and Faber, London, pp. 6770.

Franklin, M & White, I, 1991, 'The history and politics of Aboriginal health' in The Health of Aboriginal Australia, eds. J Reid & P Trompf, Harcourt Brace Jovanovich Publishers, London.

Goddard, C, 1992, *Pitjantjatjara/Yankunytjatjara to English Dictionary,* complied by Cliff Goddard, IAD Press, Alice Springs, pp. 163 & 223.

Green, J, Woods, G and Foley, B, 2011, 'Looking at language: Appropriate design for sign language resources in remote Australian Indigenous communities' in N Thieberger, L Barwick, R Billington and J Vaughen (eds.), *Sustainable data from digital research: Humanities perspective on digital research,* University of Melbourne, Custom Book Centre, Melbourne, pp. 66–89.

Haebich, A, 2001, 'A boy's short life' in *Broken circles – Fragmenting Indigenous Families 1800-2000,* Fremantle Arts Centre Press, Fremantle, pp. 17-48.

Hampton, S & Llewellyn, K (eds.), 1986, *The Penguin Book of Australian Women Poets,* Penguin Books, Melbourne.

Harris, J, 1990, *One Blood 200 Years of Aboriginal Encounter with Christianity: A Story of Hope,* Albatross Books, Sydney, pp. 385-9.

Henson, B, 1992, *A Straight-out man: FW Albrecht and Central Australian Aborigines,* Melbourne University Press, Melbourne.

Hill, B, 2003 (2002), *Broken Song – TGH Strehlow and Aboriginal Possession,* Vintage, Sydney.

Hill, B, 2001, *The Inland Sea,* Salt, London, pp. 82, 86 & 93.

Isaacs, J, 1987, *Bush Food; Aboriginal Food and Herbal Medicine,* Weldons Publishing, Sydney, p. 210.

Issacs, J, 1984, *Arts of the Dreaming: Australia's Living Heritage,* Lansdowne, Sydney, p. 241.

James, D, 2009, *Painting the song – Kaltjiti artists of the sand dune country,* McCulloch & McCulloch with Kaltjiti Arts, p. 20.

Jones, P, 2002, 'Strehlow, Theodor George Henry (Ted) (1908-1978)' in *Australian Dictionary of Biography,* National Centre of Biography, Australian National University, Canberra.

Keats, J, 1891, The Letters of John Keats, ed. S Colvin, MacMillan & Co., London.

Kitzinger, S, 1982, *Pregnancy and Childbirth,* Doubleday, London, pp. 339-40.

Latz, P, 1995, *Bushfires and Bushtucker Aboriginal Plant use in Central Australia,* IAD Press, Alice Springs, pp. 176-7.

Layton, R, 1986, *Uluru: An Aboriginal History of Ayers Rock,* Aboriginal Studies Press, Canberra, pp. 5 & 456.

Marcus, J, 2005 (2001), *This Indomitable Miss Pink – A life in Anthropology,* UNSW Press, Sydney.

Markus, A, 1990, *Governing Savages,* Allen & Unwin, Sydney.

McNally, W, 1981, *Aborigines and Artifacts,* Lutheran Publishing House, Adelaide, pp. 42-3.

Paisley, F, 2000, *Loving Protection? Australian Feminism and Aboriginal Women's Rights 1919-1939*, MUP, Melbourne, pp. 20 & 32.

Powell, A, 2009, *Far Country: A Short History of the Northern Territory*, Charles Darwin University Press, Darwin, (5th Edition).

San Roque, C, Dowd, A & Tacey, D, 2011, *Placing Psyche: Exploring Cultural Complexes in Australia*, Spring Journal Books, New Orleans.

Turpin, M, 2004, 'Have you ever wondered why Arrernte is spelt the way it is?' Central Lands Council, Alice Springs.

Westbury, D, 2002, 'Luke' in *Flying Blind*, Brandl & Schleslinger, Blackheath, p. 63.

Yates, WB, 2010 (1997), 'When you are old' in *WB Yeats Selected Poems*, ed. J Kelly, Phoenix Books. London, first published in *The Rose* (1893).

Acknowledgements

Like Bertha's travels across the desert, the process of writing her story has taken me on a long journey and through many landscapes. I appreciate the opportunities to share Bertha's poems at writing events and festivals organised by the Northern Territory Writers' Centre and other community organisations in Alice Springs and Darwin.

Poems from Walking with camels have previously appeared in the *Northern Territory Literary Awards* publications, the *Centralian Advocate*, *The Red Room Company*, *Swamp Writing*, *Axon Journal*, in *Coolabah Journal of Australian Studies*, *Communion*, *Plumwood Mountain*, and in *Underneath* – the University of Canberra Poetry Prize, and in *DiscoverySCU*. Excerpts were presented in 'Creative Manoeuvres', AAWP Conference Canberra, 2013 and at 'Watershed Conference' at the Australian Studies Centre, Universitat de Barcelona, Spain, 2014 and at the Northern Territory Writers Festival, Alice Springs, 2017.

I gratefully acknowledge the traditional owners of Kaltukatjara (Docker River) and the Central Lands Council for permission to travel to the Petermann Ranges where many of Bertha's poems were written. I acknowledge too, with thanks and gratitude, the traditional owners of Alice Springs (Mparntwe), the Arrernte people.

The Strehlow Research Centre in Alice Springs gave me enthusiastic support and unlimited access to their research library. For the many enjoyable conversations, I am grateful to John Strehlow and to Graeme Shaughnessy. My thanks to SRC for permission to reproduce the photographs: 'three camels' photographed by Bertha Strehlow, the remaining photographs by Ted Strehlow.

The support and guidance I received from the dedicated lecturers of the School of Arts & Social Science at Southern Cross University (SCU) was invaluable throughout the development and growth of Bertha's story. I appreciate the support of Central Queensland University (CQU) and La Trobe University in the early stages of the writing.

To my generous friends who shared in the growth of Bertha's story and read early versions of the story, my thanks especially to Deb Westbury, Mary Anne Butler, Meg Mooney, Sue Fielding, Glenn Morrison, Dani Powell, Jenny Taylor, Shari Kocher, Jo Dutton, Janet Hutchinson, Anne Correy, Craig San Roche, Lisa Jacobson and Penny Drysdale.

I was fortunate to receive funding from a number of sources whilst writing. My thanks to CQU and SCU for an APA scholarship; Northern Territory Department of Tourism and Culture for a writing development grant and a history grant; and to Varuna – The National Writers' House, for funds to travel to the Blue Mountains and for awarding a fellowship to the Tyrone Guthrie Centre in Ireland, where much of the editing was completed. Whilst in Ireland, I had support from generous poets and artists, my thanks especially to Mara Adamitz Scrupe, Pat Kennan and Enda Wyley.

My sister Pam French has brought Bertha's poetry to life with a series of ink drawings. I am grateful for our trips into the desert following the map of Bertha's journey, for developing our work together, and for the exhibitions that have followed.

I am grateful to my children and my large and loving family for their support of my writing, and for travelling with me on Bertha's journey. My heart and love especially, goes to Chris who has been with me every step of the way.

Finally, my thanks and gratitude to Terri-ann White for all her support and to the wonderful team at UWAP.

Printed in Australia
Ingram Content Group Australia Pty Ltd
AUHW021337181024
401468AU00002B/4

9 781742 589701